The Midnight Song

Anita Pearce

THE MIDNIGHT SONG
Copyright © 2019 by Anita Pearce

Printed in Canada
ISBN: 978-1-4866-1773-9

Word Alive Press
119 De Baets Street Winnipeg, MB R2J 3R9
www.wordalivepress.ca

Cataloguing in Publication information can be obtained from Library and Archives Canada.

Dedicated to the memory of my brothers,
Wesley and Allan Pearce.
Their faithfulness and passion for Christ
greatly influenced my life.

Contents

Acknowledgments

As I endeavor to fulfill the purposes God has placed in my heart, I'm profoundly indebted to those who have come alongside to help me. I'm particularly grateful for the self-sacrifice of friends who care about this book. They have willingly invested time and talent to produce excellence. I am deeply grateful to:

Alice Dutcyvich, your patience and perseverance amaze me. Your listening ear and gentle advice inspire me to reach beyond my limitations. It has brought joy knowing that you share the vision and enthusiasm of this project. I have great admiration for your faithful, practical walk and witness for Christ. Thank you for your friendship and encouragement.

Darlene Kienle, your faithful friendship has been one of God's greatest blessings in my life. I'm grateful for your insightful advice as we have shared thoughts and aspirations. Your approval on the projects has brought great affirmation to me. Together we pursue Christ.

Doreen Holdworth, your editing expertise has been invaluable. Years of experience have honed your skills. Your talent and perception have brought improvement and clarity. We share the passion to exalt the Lord.

The board of Inspiration Ministries, thank you for your support and encouragement. You have continually challenged me to invest all abilities for God's glory and to use every opportunity to expand the Kingdom of God.

The Word Alive staff, your wonderful team has supported and encouraged me every step of the way. Thank you for your patience with my panics! I'm grateful for your consistent cheerfulness in answering my questions, your support during this venture, and the excellence of production. It has been my pleasure to work with you.

Introduction

The hot, humid atmosphere was oppressive—sweltering, stuffy, and stale. I struggled to settle in the narrow, damp bed. Although I was exhausted, a thousand thoughts swirled in my mind. Questions, uncertainties, and anxieties filled my heart with dread. I was very alone, with no one in whom I could confide. I was in a strange land on one of my first mission trips. There had been some hostility towards the gospel, and there was no other place for me to go and no one with whom to share my distress except the Lord.

Unexpectedly from deep within, the melody of an old hymn began to surface. At first, I couldn't remember all the words, but as I began to meditate on the song, the lyrics returned.

Fear thou not, for I am with thee.
I will still thy Pilot be.
Never mind these tossing billows,
Take My hand, and trust in Me.[1]

It was as though God Himself was speaking to my heart through the words of the song. Tense muscles slowly relaxed, my

[1] Emily Devine Wilson, "I Will Pilot Thee," accessed October 1, 2018, http://www.hymntime.com/tch/bio/w/i/l/s/wilson_ed.htm.

racing mind became calm, and soothing peace filled the room. Over and over the song sang in my soul. Tears of gratitude began to flow. Clouds of fear and anxiety dissipated. My heart filled with hope to face the future. Somehow the Lord would direct, strengthen, and keep me in His care.

Since that night many years ago, He has never failed to hold my hand and pilot me safely through every storm. The Lord can also give you a song, a midnight song, to sustain you till the dawning of the new day

Chapter One

FOUNDATION FOR OUR FAITH

A group of children were playing together on the beach. With toy shovels and pails, they busied themselves constructing a castle. It was first-class with walls, towers, turrets, and even a moat. Slowly, almost imperceptibly, however, the tide moved in. The waves soon reached their castle, and within a short time it had all vanished, washed away by the ocean currents.

All around us, we can see those who spend their lives building castles in the sand. They seek security in political systems, possessions, positions, and pleasures. They spare nothing to invest in selfish indulgence, but when their lives are over, it's all swept away—just so much sand on the beach of time.

Rather than meaninglessness and vanity, the gospel of Jesus Christ proclaims revolutionary truth. The Word of God is a sure foundation, a shelter, a strong tower, and a place of eternal security.

In Matthew 24:35, Jesus makes this astonishing affirmation: "*Heaven and earth will pass away, but My words will by no means pass away.*" He announces that even though the entire world may one day be destroyed, the Word of God will stand forever.

Since the time Jesus spoke those words until now, millions of souls have found comfort in the security of God's Word, as stated well in the eighteenth-century hymn written by Edward Mote:

> My hope is built on nothing less
> Than Jesus' blood and righteousness;
> I dare not trust the sweetest frame,
> But wholly lean on Jesus' name.
> On Christ, the solid Rock, I stand,
> All other ground is sinking sand.[2]

What you read between the covers of your Bible is wisdom for a lifetime, rock-solid, forever truth—truth you can stand on, live by, and trust . . . forever.[3]

—Elizabeth George

---

[2] Edward Mote, "My Hope Is Built on Nothing Less," accessed September 25, 2018, http://www.lutheran-hymnal.com/lyrics/tlh370.htm.

[3] "Solid Quotes," goodreads, accessed September 25, 2018, https://www.goodreads.com/quotes/tag/solid.

During the Second World War, the Nazi regime used forced labor to build bunkers along the coast of France as a line of defense against Allied invasion. Some were constructed deep into the cliffs that overlook the sea; however, those in the vicinity of Dunkirk were settled on the sand dunes along the edge of the sea. In this area there were few rocks and no cliffs. During the decades since the war, those bunkers that weren't destroyed outright by the Allies have been left to ruin and crumble in the elements.

Walking along the beach, I could see the gigantic cement structures, some nearly thirty meters high, eroded by the waves and tides working the shifting sands. Now like giant toy blocks they lay strewn, cast about, and upended on the shore.

In a parable recorded in Matthew 7:24–27, Jesus contrasts the results produced by the type of foundations we build our lives upon:

> *Therefore whoever hears these sayings of Mine, and does them, I will liken him to a wise man who built his house on the rock: and the rain descended, the floods came, and the winds blew and beat on that house; and it did not fall, for it was founded on the rock. But everyone who hears these sayings of Mine, and does not do them, will be like a foolish man who built his house on the sand: and the rain descended, the floods came, and the winds blew and beat on that house; and it fell. And great was its fall.*

We build on the sure foundation only by hearing and obeying God's Word. Then when the storms of life hit, we won't fall apart and crumble in a heap. We'll stand strong, totally secure in the Christ upon whom we have taken the time to consistently build our lives. He will hold us firm.

There are established absolutes that control life, health, science, mathematics, and all that exists. For example, airplanes fly by the consistent laws of aerodynamics. These immutable and unchanging laws cannot be compromised or the plane will crash. In mathematics, two plus two always equals four.

Some people say there are many ways to God, but in Acts 4:12 we read: "*Nor is there salvation in any other, for there is no other name under heaven given among men by which we must be saved.*" This absolute truth assures our unending hope. In a world adrift in a sea of confusion and despair, we dwell safely upon the rock, the Son of God. How grateful I am that through Christ Jesus we can experience peace with God and know His personal presence in our lives.

Because God is absolute truth, I will believe what He says and live accordingly.[4]

—Bill Bright

[4] Bill Bright, "A Priceless Inheritance," CRU, accessed September 25, 2018, https://www.cru.org/us/en/train-and-grow/discover-god/god-is-absolute-truth.html.

Someone asked a well-known minister, "If the blood of Jesus is powerful enough to save the world, why are there so many sinners?"

The minister replied, "There is much soap in the world. Why are there so many dirty people? The soap on the shelf doesn't wash the people. It must be applied to do the work. It is the same with the gospel. It presents the message of forgiveness, hope, and grace that we may know in a personal relationship with Jesus Christ."

I'm amazed that the whole world doesn't run to Him. People use many excuses for not coming to Christ. All of them are rooted in the desire to live for themselves and be their own master. They live blinded by their own selfishness and rebel against the One who offered His shed blood to redeem them from rebellion and pride. Jesus offers a transformed life. We can find forgiveness and freedom from sin.

The story is told of a young girl who was very fond of her plastic necklace. When her father returned after a long journey, he held her on his knee and asked her to give him her precious necklace. At first, she refused, shaking her head and declaring how much she loved her treasure. Finally, with great reluctance, she removed it from around her neck and placed it in his open palm. Reaching into his pocket, he took out a little box. When she opened it, she discovered a new necklace made of real pearls! What a great exchange!

Multitudes hold tightly to the plastic counterfeits offered by the momentary pleasures of sin, yet Christ offers us infinite treasure in exchange for our useless, broken toys. He has done everything to provide for our forgiveness and salvation. We can know His transformation when we surrender our sin and receive Him personally.

In 1 Corinthians 1:18, the apostle Paul declares, *"For the message of the cross is foolishness to those who are perishing, but to us who are being saved it is the power of God."* The message of the cross has always provoked mockery and offence. For some it seems simplistic; for others, tragic. It always offends those who trust in their personal morality for righteousness. The cross presents humanity with an undeniable dilemma and decision. Ultimately, however, it provides the only way of salvation.

The message of the death, resurrection, and eternal lordship of Jesus alone can transform the human heart. Through repentance and faith, the message of the cross brings forgiveness for our sins, freedom from sin's grip, and fulfillment in God's design.

&

It was Christ who willingly went to the cross, and it was our sins that took Him there.[5]

—Franklin Graham

[5] "19 Important Quotes about the Cross," Christian Quotes, accessed September 25, 2018, https://www.christianquotes.info/top-quotes/19-important-quotes-about-the-cross/#ixzz5K8ecg3C4.

The evening service was to be in the town thirty-five kilometers away. Everything was well organized and packed in the car in excellent time. In fact, my effective planning meant I would arrive early. I was priding myself on my efficiency as I drove along. Then one kilometer from the church, I realized I had forgotten the key! There was absolutely no honest way into that building without that five-centimeter piece of metal! There was no recourse but to return the thirty-five kilometers, get the key, drive like fury, and arrive very nearly late.

Jesus declared, *"I am the way, the truth, and the life. No one comes to the Father except through Me"* (John 14:6). He made it clear there are not many ways to God—only one. He is the key. Some may suggest that this scripture is intolerant, too narrow-minded, or even bigoted. Every time I get in an airplane, I realize that the principles of aerodynamics are also intolerant. To break those laws will crash the plane! There are countless illustrations to prove only one key fits the lock; the principle will never change.

Truth is principle—unalterable, eternal, the very character of God revealed in Jesus Christ. Every human heart stands before its own conscience either in repentance or condemnation at the revelation that Jesus is the only way to God.

In Psalm 119, the longest chapter of the Bible, the writer expresses his love for the Word of God. Satan, aligned with the world, has assaulted and insulted God's holy Word. For centuries it has been burned and spurned in attempts to destroy it, yet it always rises and rules in triumph. Within its pages we find the immutable laws of God. Its living message of hope, direction, and comfort exudes life-changing power. More than ever we need to read, study, and fill our hearts with Bible truth. It will sustain us in troubled days. It is written, *"Your word I have hidden in my heart, that I might not sin against You"* (Psalm119:11). Someone said, "Sin will keep us from this book; this book will keep us from sin."

❧

Within the covers of the Bible are the answers for all the problems men face.[6]

—Ronald Reagan

[6] "Bible Quotes," BrainyQuote, accessed September 25, 2018, https://www.brainyquote.com/topics/bible.

On a Saturday morning one summer, I walked down the street of a small town. In the space of only a few blocks, I passed about a dozen garage sales. Tables were piled high with clothes, toys, useless trinkets, and general junk. Crowds of people vied for the nickel and dime sales, and packed shopping bags with assortments of odds and ends. Many would take their treasures home to add to their already overstuffed collections. In some cases, they would be put into the next garage sale!

Although we all appreciate a good bargain and need useful items, we must be aware of the treachery of materialism. Why do we want all this stuff? The more material goods we have, the more we seem to want. Then we need bigger houses to store it all! We spend our lives accumulating possessions, all of which we leave behind when we die. When someone heard that a rich man had died, the question was asked, "How much did he leave behind?" The answer came, "He left it all!"

In Luke 12:15, Jesus taught: "… *Take heed and beware of covetousness, for one's life does not consist in the abundance of the things he possesses.*" He admonished us to live simply, without covetousness. We need to lay up our treasures in heaven by investing in those priorities that will endure forever.

One of the most startling proofs of the infallibility of Scripture is the unerring accuracy of prophetic statements. In Isaiah 13, for example, the prophet Isaiah accurately describes the rise and destruction of mighty Babylon—long before Babylon even became a world power! Cyrus, King of Persia, was named several hundred years before he was even born. There were hundreds of prophecies regarding the coming of Jesus Christ, telling of His birth, His death, His resurrection, and even stating exact words He would say.

The Bible is a living book, a spiritual book, different from all others. As you read the Word of God, let your heart be opened to hear Him speak into your life and situation. David said in Psalm 119:105, "*Your word is a lamp to my feet and a light to my path.*"

I've read the last page of the Bible. It's all going to turn out all right.[7]

—Billy Graham

[7] "Bible Quotes," BrainyQuote, accessed September 25, 2018, https://www.brainyquote.com/topics/bible.

On one occasion, I was invited to attend a ceremony to honor the accomplishments of a wealthy entrepreneur. The room was filled with elegance. Fine suits and gorgeous gowns were worn by many. Everyone oozed confidence and class. The appearances of self-sufficiency and refinement displayed all the trappings of wealth. But as I sat on the sidelines and observed, I was deeply struck by the superficiality of it all. The conversations were light; the smiles were strained. Everyone seemed to be competing for significance. Although it was to be a celebration of attainment, I gazed into lonely eyes. The road to wealth was paved with shattered shards of broken homes and shallow friendships. Most serious of all, the desire for relationship with Jesus had been sacrificed for the world's acclaim.

My heart was both sad and glad as I returned to my rather humble home. I was saddened by the emptiness and waste of my friend's life in the quest for material possessions and recognition. But I was glad that I'd found the source of life itself through faith in Jesus Christ.

As the nation of Israel prepared to enter the promised land of Canaan, God gave Joshua the keys to success:

This Book of the Law shall not depart from your mouth, but you shall meditate in it day and night, that you may observe to do according to all that is written in it. For then you will make your way prosperous, and then you will have good success. (Joshua 1:8)

In the self-seeking, frenetic race to achieve temporary material possessions and worldly approval, we need to re-evaluate the essence and source of true prosperity. Obedience to God's Word, submission to His will, and accomplishment of His work will bring His favor upon our lives. To know Him, to love Him, and to live for Him—there is no greater success in this life or the life to come.

In Jeremiah 42, the people come to the prophet requesting an answer to their dilemma. They solemnly promise to obey whatever God tells them to do; however, when God's answer doesn't please them, they choose to rebel and follow their own plans. The end result is catastrophic.

How similar to our reactions on certain occasions! We may seek the Lord for answers with the underlying motive of persuading Him to bless us in what we're going to do anyway! We must open our hearts in true submission to His Word. Obedience will bring the ultimate blessing we seek.

❧

It ain't the parts of the Bible that I can't understand that bother me, it's the parts that I do understand.[8]

—Mark Twain

[8] "Quotes about the Bible:25 Awesome Sayings," What Christians Want to Know, accessed September 25, 2018, https://www.whatchristianswanttoknow.com/quotes-about-the-bible-25-awesome-sayings/#ixzz5K818TrYC.

The world watched in horror and disbelief in 2011 as images were released of the destruction caused by a magnitude nine earthquake in Japan. The ensuing tsunami brought waves peaking at over forty meters. Many people asked why God would permit this tragedy and loss of life.

In Luke 13:1–5, the same question regarding a tragedy of that era is presented to Jesus:

There were present at that season some who told Him about the Galileans whose blood Pilate had mingled with their sacrifices. And Jesus answered and said to them, "Do you suppose that these Galileans were worse sinners than all other Galileans, because they suffered such things? I tell you, no; but unless you repent you will all likewise perish. Or those eighteen on whom the tower in Siloam fell and killed them, do you think that they were worse sinners than all other men who dwelt in Jerusalem? I tell you, no; but unless you repent you will all likewise perish."

The question should not be, "Why does God permit tragedy?" but rather the exclamation, "What great mercy that any of us are spared!" We're no better or worse than those who have suffered such catastrophes. We've all broken God's laws and deserve His justice. Jesus calls us to repentance.

The only thing that counts is right relationship with Jesus Christ. Our life on this planet is a trial run in which we are to prepare for eternity. Everyone shall ultimately stand before God, the judge of all humanity. If we've been granted the grace to live, it's for His glory. We're reminded in 1 John 2:28: "*... abide in Him, that when He appears, we may have confidence and not be ashamed before Him at His coming.*"

Paul declares in Galatians 6:14, *"But God forbid that I should boast except in the cross of our Lord Jesus Christ, by whom the world has been crucified to me, and I to the world."* Paul attributed his source, his purpose, his reason to live—in fact his total satisfaction—to the cross of Jesus. His absolute motivation in life was to be totally identified with the death, burial, and resurrection of Jesus. This dimension of passionate relationship with Christ will be discovered as we lose ourselves only to find ourselves in Him alone.

Love is not just a sentiment. Love is a great controlling passion and it always expresses itself in terms of obedience.[9]

—*Martyn Lloyd-Jones*

[9] "211 Quotes about Obedience," Christian Quotes, accessed September 25, 2018, https://www.christianquotes.info/quotes-by-topic/quotes-about-obedience/#axzz5K8eIKy^k.

A pastor was counseling a couple who were experiencing marital difficulties. The relationship had been strained and communication was nearly non-existent. After several encounters, the pastor sensed some success, as both parties were beginning to speak together in the same room with him. Suddenly, the wife said something that the husband contradicted. After several moments of hot-tempered argument, her husband declared, "But I can prove you are wrong!" With that, he jumped from his chair, went into another room, and returned with a large cardboard box. Inside, neatly filed in alphabetical order, he presented the record of every mistake his wife had ever made!

Yes, he could prove his point and win the argument. But he was missing the principle of truly loving, forgiving, and caring for his wife. He was so interested in keeping the rules, he was in danger of losing his relationship and, eventually, his home and family.

The people of Israel complicated their relationship with God by adding multitudes of rules and regulations. Their spiritual condition deteriorated to the point where the people were not really worshiping God as much as their rules about Him.

With divine inspiration, the prophet Micah carefully explains that the Lord searches for pure hearts full of love for Him and their fellow men: *"He has shown you, O man, what is good; and what does the Lord require of you but to do justly, to love mercy, and to walk humbly with your God?"* (Micah 6:8).

Sometimes we're guilty of seeking the mysterious, the mountain peaks of His presence, while He is calling us to the simplicity of walking in kindness and compassion with a pure heart. Someone has dared to say, "How wonderful it would be if Christians would just be kind to one another!"

The unique power of the Bible is its ability to impart life. Although there may be many verses we don't understand with our intellect, our spiritual man is nourished. As by faith we practise its precepts, obey its commands, and meditate on its wisdom, we find practical solutions for daily dilemmas, as well as spiritual growth and stability.

The apostle Paul encourages Timothy to study the Word of God to find counsel and wisdom: "*Be diligent to present yourself approved to God, a worker who does not need to be ashamed, rightly dividing the word of truth*" (2 Timothy 2:15). Let us ask the Lord for a renewed hunger for His Word.

I believe the Bible is the best gift God has ever given to man. All the good from the Savior of the world is communicated to us through this book.[10]

—Abraham Lincoln

---

[10] "Quotes about the Bible: 25 Awesome Sayings," What Christians Want to Know, accessed September 25, 2018, https://www.whatchristianswanttoknow.com/quotes-about-the-bible-25-awesome-sayings/.

I like my compact digital camera because I just have to point and push the button to take a picture. A friend pointed out the tremendous potential of the camera. If I read the instruction book, I could learn all the amazing features and possibilities and produce high quality pictures. Those features don't particularly interest me, because I prefer simplicity … probably because I simply can't be bothered to study the manual!

God gives us many great truths in His Word. Many of us, however, are content to go through life with minimal understanding of the Bible. The Lord has great treasures to share with us. In 2 Timothy 3:16–17, we're told: *"All Scripture is given by inspiration of God, and is profitable for doctrine, for reproof, for correction, for instruction in righteousness, that the man of God may be complete, thoroughly equipped for every good work."* If we would open our hearts to Him and study His Word, we would discover the riches of His kingdom.

Chapter Two

Direction for the Day

A rriving at the intersection on the mountain road, I was unsure of which way to go. In both directions the forest obliterated the view. I couldn't see road signs anywhere. Now was the moment to turn on my GPS! From a satellite in outer space, my position was determined. In just a moment, I knew exactly where I was supposed to go. The way was clear; the directions were marked. All I had to do was follow the voice. Sure enough, I arrived safely at my destination.

When uncertainty fills our lives, we can connect to the Lord, who knows exactly where we are! He can speak within our hearts, assuring us of His love and care. As we follow His voice and obey His Word, He will guide us safely home.

In John 4:4, we read that Jesus was compelled by His Father to travel through Samaria on His way from Judea to Galilee. He had an appointment to speak to a Samaritan woman—an encounter that would ultimately change her life. Later, in Acts 8, we read how God sent Philip to explain the gospel to the Ethiopian finance minister, who was returning home from a Jewish feast in Jerusalem. That man in turn took this marvelous message home to his people, resulting in the nation being powerfully affected by the gospel.

We must not underrate the purposes of God. The Lord saw the hunger of these hearts. Faithful and obedient witnesses planted gospel seeds. Individuals who may have seemed insignificant became pivotal people in changing nations. Never underestimate the value of one soul or the worth of one seed.

❧

All the flowers of all the tomorrows are in the seeds of today.[11]

—Robin Craig Clark

---

[11] "Robin Craig Clark," goodreads, accessed September 25, 2018, https://www.goodreads.com/quotes/8893158-all-the-flowers-of-all-the-tomorrows-are-in-the.

The day I arrived in their town, the family with whom it had been arranged for me to stay were all sick with the flu. As a result, in a completely unforeseen arrangement, I was invited to lunch with another woman. In a short time, I discovered she was a very religious person with an earnest desire to do what was right, but who had never come to a living, personal relationship with Christ. From the Word of God, I was able to show her the way to repentance and faith in Jesus. I witnessed the power of the Holy Spirit as He brought the assurance of His presence into her heart. Without the last-minute change of plans, I probably never would have had the opportunity to speak personally with this precious lady. She may never have understood the simplicity of the gospel, and I would have missed one of those thrilling moments of watching a life transformed by God's power.

The life lesson is that every footstep of the child of God is directed by our loving Savior to bring glory to Him. Nothing happens by accident. Someone has said that coincidences are actually God at work in disguise. Interruptions to our plans, surprise circumstances, even inconveniences could be God's orchestrations to put us in exactly the right place at the right time.

What a difference perspective can make! When the armies of Israel looked at Goliath, they saw him as a terrifying enemy of enormous stature with dangerous weapons. But when David looked at him, he saw him through the eyes of faith. Goliath was merely a big mouth defying the name of the Most High God. While everyone said, "The giant is too big to overcome," David declared, "He's so big, I can't miss!" Whatever the impossible obstacles in your life, let the Lord open your eyes of faith to see His perspective. God is bigger than your problem!

The essence of optimism is that it takes no account of the present, but it is a source of inspiration, of vitality and hope where others have resigned; it enables a man to hold his head high, to claim the future for himself and not to abandon it to his enemy.[12]

—Dietrich Bonhoeffer

[12] Christian Quotes, accessed September 25, 2018, https://www.christianquotes.info/search-for-a-quote/#ixzz5PlnyupiA.

While I was in the Canadian Arctic in the month of February, it was the coldest it had been for many years. Wind chills measured -65C. Worship services had been arranged in a remote village accessible only by air. After several delays, I was finally able to fly in for three days of scheduled services. Then the storm came.

For three days and nights, powerful ninety-kilometer winds swept the snow into huge, hard drifts. Visibility was zero. Driven snow pellets were blinding. No airplanes could fly—not even emergency flights. Businessmen, tourists, and hunters were all stranded where the blizzard caught them. Frost and snow covered the windows of the cozy, warm room where I was staying.

In spite of the cold and storm, many folks came to the services every evening. The well-built church was bright, warm, and filled with the presence of the Lord. Hearts were challenged and encouraged as we worshiped God together. For some it was a moment of powerful encounter with the Lord.

Although the storm was serious, I had a great awareness that I was exactly where I was supposed to be, and a strong assurance that I would leave when I had accomplished the mission God had given me. Sure enough, the day I was scheduled to leave dawned bright and clear. As the airplane lifted above the tundra, I marveled at the peace of the Lord and His direction in the finest details.

We aren't left alone to struggle though the storms of life. God's guiding hand is directing our lives according to His infinite plan. Looking back with amazement, we can see His love and care for us all along the way.

Where we look is absolutely crucial, because that's ultimately where we go. Whatever we're concentrating on will be reproduced by our emotions, words, and actions. When we center our lives on the Word of God, its principles will become our priorities. In Psalm 25:15, David writes, "*My eyes are ever toward the Lord, for He shall pluck my feet out of the net.*"

Some people focus on their circumstances, health, money, or work. We find this warning in Proverbs 23:5: "*Will you set your eyes on that which is not? For riches certainly make themselves wings; they fly away like an eagle toward heaven.*" Some folks are consumed with themselves and their activities. We need to carefully evaluate the consequences and aim for higher goals. David also writes, "*I have set the Lord always before me; because He is at my right hand I shall not be moved*" (Psalm 16:8).

It's not what you look at that matters, it's what you see.[13]

—Henry David Thoreau

[13] "Vision Quotes," AZ Quotes, accessed September 25, 2018, http://www.azquotes.com/topics/vision.html.

An acquaintance was learning to drive the car. She needed practice, however, especially with parking. On a quiet Sunday afternoon, her husband suggested she take the car to the local shopping mall. The stores were closed for the day, and there was a large, open parking lot where she could drive about by herself to gain confidence. He carefully reminded her of one large lamp post in the middle of the four-hectare parking lot. "Whatever you do," he laughed as she drove away, "don't hit the light post!" Conscious of his warning, she set out. After a short time, she succeeded in accomplishing the near impossible. She hit the post! She ran into the single obstacle in four hectares! It's a basic principle—we go in the direction we look.

When I was learning to drive, my older brother reminded me to keep my eyes on the road. He told me, "If you're distracted by the scenery, you'll become the scenery!" We can be bombarded by constant distractions drawing our attention away from God and away from what is true and pure. James described this process: "*But each one is tempted when he is drawn away by his own desires and enticed*" (James 1:14). Keep your heart and eyes centered on Jesus Christ. Ignore the countless pressures to be turned aside. Then you will be able to clearly see the way forward.

The Lord has given us a tremendous gift—the gift of choice. Although our circumstances may be less than ideal, we can always choose our attitudes, actions, and responses. Moses summarized this challenge to the people of Israel in Deuteronomy 30:19: "*I call heaven and earth as witnesses today against you, that I have set before you life and death, blessing and cursing; therefore choose life, that both you and your descendants may live …*" He encouraged the people to make the choices resulting in life and blessing.

It's easy to blame our problems on God, people, or the devil. We can resign ourselves to discouragement and despair; however, we can make the choice to be a victor instead of a victim. Instead of searching for excuses, we can seek solutions. In the darkness of our night, we can still choose to triumph.

Destiny is no matter of chance. It is a matter of choice. It is not a thing to be waited for, it is a thing to be achieved.[14]

—William Jennings Bryan

---

[14] "William Jennings Bryan Quotes," BrainyQuote, accessed September 25, 2018, https://www. brainyquote.com/authors/william_jennings_bryan.

On occasion I've volunteered to sing at a nearby retirement home. In the community room the staff set up a large bird cage, which has become popular with many residents. The canaries are very alert, and their cheerful chirps echo through the halls of the home. I've noticed, however, that while I'm playing and singing, they become especially animated. They all pause on their perches and sing with all their might. Their delightful, trilling voices are heard over everyone as they joyfully harmonize.

These bright, cheery birds were meant to fly free in the wild, but now, through no fault of their own, they find themselves captured and held in the cage. Instead of bemoaning their situation, they sing their hearts out, not realizing how much joy they bring to all who are listening.

Perhaps you find yourself trapped by unwelcome circumstances, held in an uncomfortable place. Situations beyond your control are dictating your present position. You may not have chosen your circumstance, but you can decide your response. Remember— even a bird in a cage can choose to sing!

During the times when we don't see the answer to our prayers, we may be tempted to become discouraged. Patience is a virtue that is far easier to discuss than to possess! It's often closely related to perseverance.

In Hebrews 10:35–36, we're reminded: "*Therefore do not cast away your confidence, which has great reward. For you have need of endurance, so that after you have done the will of God, you may receive the promise.*" God's ways are not our ways, and His time is not our time. Let's stand firm with patience and perseverance, trusting God to work His solutions for His glory in our lives.

Patience is not simply the ability to wait—it's how we behave while we're waiting.[15]

—Joyce Meyer

---

[15] "Top 10 Patience Quotes," BrainyQuote, accessed September 25, 2018, https://www.brainyquote.com/lists/topics/top_10_patience_quotes.

It had been a very long day with nearly ten hours of steady driving. As I neared a small city, I began to look for a hotel where I could stop for the night. To my dismay, most were displaying "No Vacancy" signs. There was one more hotel to try, somewhat higher class than I thought my budget would allow. The clerk informed me that they were also filled up.

As I got back into my car, the hotel manager suddenly appeared at my window. He said, "Actually, we do have one room left, but it's our high-end executive suite. You look like a nice lady, so I'll let you have it for a 30 percent discount." I got the last bed in the city, in the nicest hotel, at a discount! Who could resist such an offer! I also thought it a pity that Mary and Joseph had not found such a hospitable innkeeper!

As I laid my weary self under the luxurious covers, I wondered how many similar experiences had been overlooked as mere coincidences. For example, on another occasion I was driving into a new city with no address for the church where I was to speak, and I stopped by accident directly in front of it!

Another time during a long-distance journey, I heard serious noises in the back of the car. When I finally got to the garage several hundred kilometers later, I was told that "Angels must be watching over you!" Another few kilometers and I would have lost one wheel. I've experienced a multitude of similar interventions too numerous to record.

In retrospect, I recognize these are wonderful manifestations of the Lord's watchful care and gracious favor. What a tremendous blessing to know, as the psalmist David said in Psalm 31:15, "*My times are in Your hand …*"

The Amplified Bible uses powerful words to describe Jesus' invitation in Matthew 11:28–30:

Come to Me, all who are weary and heavily burdened [by religious rituals that provide no peace], and I will give you rest [refreshing your souls with salvation]. Take My yoke upon you and learn from Me, for I am gentle and humble in heart, and you will find rest (renewal, blessed quiet) for your souls. For My yoke is easy [to bear] and My burden is light.

What a great privilege to be able to simply come to Jesus with our burdens. When we cast our care upon Him, He lifts the heavy load. Walking in His way brings rest and refreshing.

Our anxiety does not empty tomorrow of its sorrows, but only empties today of its strengths.[16]
—Charles Haddon Spurgeon

[16] "Anxiety Quotes," goodreads, accessed September 25, 2018, https://www.goodreads.com/quotes/tag/anxiety.

The schedule demanded an eight-hour drive between locations. I got an early start but began to hear radio announcements regarding a severe snowstorm along the route I was to take. Although I was concentrating on the road, I somehow missed the intersection where I was to follow the highway eastward. After about thirty kilometers, I realized my mistake. Instead of returning to the original highway, I took a secondary road. What I thought was a mistake turned out to be divine intervention.

Within minutes of turning east on the smaller highway, I experienced the full fury of the winter storm. The next several hours I drove onwards, white-knuckled through virtual white-outs in heavy-falling, hard-blowing snow. The mild temperatures made the road greasy-slick as the snow turned to ice beneath my tires. In other places, my trusty van crawled over half-meter drifts. Finally, I was able to stop in a village and take refuge at the home of a good friend. We shared a beautiful evening safe within her cozy house.

The storm passed, and early in the morning I continued on my way. As I came to the original highway, I could see dozens of heavy trucks and cars lining the road. Later that day, my friend emailed me the news. In the intense storm, two semi-trailers had collided, creating a sixteen-car pileup. The highway had been closed by the police. Rescuers and ambulances had taken several hours in near-zero visibility to get the people out of the mess to the nearest hospital. About a hundred people had been taken to a local school gymnasium for the night. Had I not missed that road, I would very possibly have been in the middle of those accidents, or worse. God directs us even when we're unaware of His intervention.

In 2 Timothy 3:13, Paul warns of troubled days ahead. He declares, *"But evil men and impostors will grow worse and worse, deceiving and being deceived."* With every newscast I watch I wonder how much deeper society will descend into darkness and deception. How long before the judge of all mankind says "enough" and His judgment comes to a world that has rejected Him? Paul adds in 2 Timothy 3:14: *"But you must continue in the things which you have learned and been assured of, knowing from whom you have learned them ..."* He challenges believers to beware of deception and deceivers, to be faithful, to be steadfast, and to stand true.

ᔕ

Whatever your heart clings to and confides in, that is really your God.[17]

—Martin Luther

[17] "91 Quotes about Temptation," Christian Quotes, accessed September 25, 2018, https://www.christianquotes.info/quotes-by-topic/quotes-about-temptation/#axzz5K8eIKy6k.

I sauntered along a country path, thoroughly enjoying the bright sunshine and warm weather. I was momentarily distracted by some beautiful wildflowers on the other side of the barbed wire fence, so I bent over the fence for a closer look. I gingerly pushed the wire down, studiously avoiding the barbs. At that same moment, my foot caught on a tree root.

As graceful as a swan diving into a mud puddle, I upended, somersaulting clear over the fence, and landed in a spectacular heap on the other side. With a couple of minor punctures to my skin and my pride, I sat rather deflated in the long grass. The gorgeous flowers were completely flattened!

I'd been very careful touching the fence but hadn't paid attention to the small, protruding root. Many of the major stumbles in our lives are caused by seemingly insignificant issues that catch us off guard. Sometimes we find the original distraction, which seemed so beautiful and worthwhile, to be flat and of little value. We easily recognize large obstacles and roadblocks, but we must watch for the snares that would trip us up along the way. We must not be distracted from the clear path God has given us to walk. Let us keep our eyes fixed on the Lord.

In Acts 4:36, we're told about "… *Joses, who was also named Barnabas by the apostles (which is translated Son of Encouragement) …*" What a tremendous reputation and reflection of this man's character!

Society is filled with depressing situations and difficult circumstances. On every side are voices that tear down, corrupt, destroy, and discourage. Let us stand against the current and be messengers of hope in Christ. We can be the voice bringing fresh courage and comfort from God's promises. May the Lord help us take the challenge and become known as encouragers—speaking uplifting words, performing unselfish acts, and reaching out with greater empathy to those in need.

Resolve to be tender with the young, compassionate with the aged, sympathetic with the striving, and tolerant of the weak and wrong. Sometime in life you will have been all of these.[18]

—George Washington Carver

[18] "Empathy Quotes," goodreads, accessed September 25, 2018, https://www.goodreads.com/quotes/tag/empathy.

B ethlehem was bursting with weary pilgrims frantically pushing through crowded streets. Caesar's call for a census had set the entire Roman Empire in motion, unintentionally ensuring Mary's baby boy would be born in Bethlehem, exactly as the prophets had foretold.

We don't know what the innkeeper was thinking as he told the heavily pregnant woman and her husband there was no room for them in the inn. He may have been so distracted by the tinkling coins filling his coffers that he failed to notice their plight, or he may have felt irritated that yet another customer had disrupted his already hectic world. Perhaps he felt sorrowful, wringing his hands with guilt as he sent them into the darkness. It may be that the manger, the village feed-box, was his desperate attempt to find them some comfort and shelter.

No, we don't know his thoughts, but they may be the mirror of our own. Seeking our own selfish pursuits, God and others may be pushed off our agendas. We may feel irritated by those who interrupt our schedules or plans. In moments of genuine compassion, we hear God's whisper urging us to touch the needy world around us. Too often out of our suppressed guilt we throw money at good causes, attempting to ease our conscience, or hoping others will do the task God has given us. The knock at the door of our heart may be the Lord Himself.

Chapter Three

SONGS FOR THE SOUL

There are multiple genres of music. We can choose between jazz, classic, country, rock, rap, blues, bluegrass, ballad, or one of a dozen other styles. Song has the ability to profoundly move our emotions, impress our thoughts, and express our deepest sentiments. It has been called a language of the soul. Music has the capacity to bring healing to a troubled mind. It has been used as therapy because of its restorative power.

In the dark struggles of fear, uncertainty, or despair, the Lord is able to give the song of hope in the soul. God's presence always brings light into our night. We can pour out our hearts in prayer, praise, and worship. In Christ we can find a new song ... in fact, He is our song!

When we submit our lives to Jesus as Savior and Lord, His power sets us free from the law of sin that had ruled us. As we daily receive His grace, choosing to live in obedience to His Word, we discover that the grip of guilt and condemnation has been broken. We are empowered to live in the consciousness of His divine forgiveness, freedom, and fulfillment. This is what Paul describes in Romans 8:1–2:

> *There is therefore now no condemnation to those who are in Christ Jesus, who do not walk according to the flesh, but according to the Spirit. For the law of the Spirit of life in Christ Jesus has made me free from the law of sin and death.*

We can live free because of what Christ has done for us.

To serve God, to love God, to enjoy God, is the sweetest freedom in the world.[19]

—Thomas Watson

[19] "63 Quotes about Freedom," Christian Quotes, accessed September 25, 2018, https://www.christianquotes.info/quotes-by-topic/quotes-about-freedom/#ixzz5K9fnOdE4.

During winter, the sap of the Canadian sugar maple descends into the roots of the tree. From the beginning of February until the end of March, it returns up into the trunk, preparing for the summer season. When it begins to flow, small holes are drilled in the side of the trees, into which a short pipe is inserted. The sap is collected, either in pails or by a network of pipes draining into large vats. It's then boiled, turning it into syrup through the process of evaporation. On average it takes forty liters of sap to make one liter of delicious maple syrup. The thin, diluted raw sap has a very mild flavor; however, after heat has been applied, it yields the purest maple syrup with the richest savor.

As I reflected on this process, I thought about the refining work God does in our hearts. Although we greatly dislike the heat of pressure and trials in our lives, that's what helps to develop the deepest pools of character and dependency upon God. Through this refining process, much dross is removed, and the most important values remain. Those around us can then be refreshed with our courage and joy. We must not fret against the pressures but yield to the purifying heat, allowing the Lord to produce His character within.

During the reign of King Jehoshaphat, several surrounding armies joined forces to attack the nation of Judah. The king and his people were frankly terrified. As they called on God for help, God sent a prophet with words of encouragement. Following the Lord's direction, Jehoshaphat summoned the priests to prepare to face the advancing armies—with the weapon of worship! We read the amazing result:

> … he appointed those who should sing to the Lord, and who should praise the beauty of holiness, as they went out before the army and were saying: "Praise the Lord, for His mercy endures forever." Now when they began to sing and to praise, the Lord set ambushes against the people of Ammon, Moab, and Mount Seir, who had come against Judah; and they were defeated. (2 Chronicles 20:21–22)

Prayer and praise are powerful tools at the disposal of all who will call on the name of the Lord. When we express our dependence upon God and offer thanksgiving for His faithfulness, everything changes. Our attitudes are altered; we are transformed!

We would worry less if we praised more. Thanksgiving is the enemy of discontent and dissatisfaction.[20]

—Harry Ironside

[20] "20 Glorious Quotes about Praise," Christian Quotes, accessed September 25, 2018, https://www.christianquotes.info/top-quotes/20-glorious-quotes-about-praise/#ixzz5KP5eTTyY.

The darkness of the night reflected the somberness of the nation. For over four hundred years, the prophets of God had been silent. There had been no voice, no vision. There had been great turbulence as warring factions tried to subdue and subvert the people of Israel. Being at the crossroads of major trading routes, Rome had taken an interest in conquering the land and was now occupying Israel. They enslaved and exploited the people.

As shepherds sat in the darkness on the hillside tending their sheep, they were aware of the painful political situation. Gloom and hopelessness pervaded the land. There was even doubt in the credibility of God's promises. Where was their Messiah? Where was God in this obscurity? Suddenly, in the blackness—a light shone brightly! Angelic hosts filled the sky with song. They spoke of peace and hope. The Messiah had come!

Perhaps your world is filled with darkness. Hope seems far away. Doubts are damaging your faith in God's promises. Stop! Look up! Listen! Stop concentrating on your disappointment. See what God is doing; hear what God is saying. He is mightily at work. Even now, the preparations for your answer are on the way. Angels are about to sing. In the night, you will hear the song of hope again.

In John 15:5, Jesus reminds us of the importance of our connection with Him: "*I am the vine, you are the branches. He who abides in Me, and I in him, bears much fruit; for without Me you can do nothing.*" It's impossible for a severed branch to be productive. In the same way, without a living relationship with Jesus, our spirit will wither and dry.

When everything is going well, it's easy to become independent, self-righteous, and self-reliant. We must continually return and recognize everything in our life is from Him, by Him, and to Him.

Trying to be happy without a sense of God's presence is like trying to have a bright day without the sun.[21]

—A. W. Tozer

---

[21] "Dependence on God," Daily Christian Quotes, June 16, 2018, accessed September 25, 2018, https://www.dailychristianquote.com/tag/dependence-on-god/.

Together with fellow Canadian citizens, I attended the annual Remembrance Day service. We solemnly sang our national anthem then paused for a moment of silence beside the cenotaph erected in the park many years ago. The names of the local boys who had died in the service of our country were engraved on the bronze plaque above the words, "Lest we forget."

The book of Deuteronomy summarizes the last words of Moses to the people of Israel. For forty years he had faithfully led them out of Egypt and through the wilderness. He had taught them God's laws, instructing them in the ways of righteousness. He knows he will no longer lead them as they cross the Jordan River to inherit the land of Canaan. In his last discourse, he implores them not to forget all that the Lord has done for them and all that they have learned of His ways.

At least eight times in the book of Deuteronomy he challenges the people: "... *when you have eaten and are full—then beware, lest you forget the Lord who brought you out of the land of Egypt ...*" (Deuteronomy 6:11–12). When everything goes well, how quickly, how easily, we forget the blessings received from the Lord—answers to prayer and lessons learned. He has shown His goodness and faithfulness to us. Recognizing His mercy and kindness, we should consciously and continually thank God.

In Numbers 23:19, the Bible declares: "*God is not a man, that He should lie, nor a son of man, that He should repent. Has He said, and will He not do? Or has He spoken, and will He not make it good?*" In a world of broken promises, we find humans are often incapable of living up to expectations or fulfilling intentions. This scripture, however, assures us of God's faithfulness. His Word shall stand. His principles and promises are sure. Surrounded by turmoil, hopelessness, and uncertainty, we can find comfort and assurance in the very character of God.

In God's faithfulness lies eternal security.[22]

—Corrie Ten Boom

[22] AZ Quotes, accessed October 1, 2018, https://www.azquotes.com/quote/878014.

The trouble started when one of the bridesmaids fainted. Then the ring bearer bolted with stage fright. It took ten minutes to find the ring. The photographer was trying to get the perfect picture when he lost his balance and fell off his perch in the choir loft. During the reception, there was a power outage. Someone had the bright idea to bring candles. That worked well until one candle was knocked over, setting a tablecloth on fire. There were screams of fear and shouts for help, while quick-thinking guests threw water in all directions. It was the wedding version of Murphy's Law—everything that could go wrong, went wrong! Thankfully, it was only a comedy movie clip.

Perhaps you've experienced those times when everything seems to be collapsing at once. Your heart cries out, "What else can happen?" Even in the most difficult circumstances, we can find inner resources of strength in the Lord.

The prophet Habakkuk warned of terrible disasters about to happen to Judah because they had turned from the Lord. In spite of the impending doom, he understood that his relationship with God was secure; therefore, he could sing this song:

Though the fig tree may not blossom, nor fruit be on the vines; though the labor of the olive may fail, and the fields yield no food; though the flock may be cut off from the fold, and there be no herd in the stalls—yet I will rejoice in the Lord, I will joy in the God of my salvation. (Habakkuk 3:17–18)

When our world is turned upside down with confusion and distress at every turn, remember that nothing can separate us from Christ. We can rejoice and be grateful because:
- God is always in control.
- Through our Savior, Jesus, we can have peace with God.
- He will never leave us or forsake us.
- In Christ, our hope is eternal.

In John 4, Jesus meets a Samaritan woman drawing water from the well. He tells her:

> *Whoever drinks of this water will thirst again, but whoever drinks of the water that I shall give him will never thirst. But the water that I shall give him will become in him a fountain of water springing up into everlasting life.* (John 4:13–14)

He taught that He is the only source of lasting satisfaction. Material possessions, popular attractions, or natural achievements may bring temporary happiness or relief, but the sense of completeness is transitory. Soon the inner hunger, the heart craving, returns. Like drinking brine from the salt sea, we experience even more thirst.

Jesus identified the anguish of her heart. He explained that He could give her the solution: forgiveness of sins, freedom of conscience, and fulfillment of purpose. Then, even far beyond her wildest expectation, the presence and peace of God in her heart could satisfy her soul's hunger. She could drink deeply of Him and never be thirsty again. We can also come and drink today.

Christ is not a reservoir but a spring. His life is continual, active and ever passing on with an outflow as necessary as its inflow. If we do not perpetually draw the fresh supply from the Living Fountain, we shall either grow stagnant or empty. It is, therefore, not so much a perpetual fullness as a perpetual filling.[23]

—A.B. Simpson

23 "Christian Quotes," Christian.com, accessed September 25, 2018, http://christian-quotes. ochristian.com/christian-quotes_ochristian.cgi?query=living%20water&action=search.

While ministering in Brazil, I was invited to speak in a small church one evening. It was packed with young people and down-to-earth folks, most who had walked from the poor areas nearby. The service was simple, the worship genuine, and the spiritual hunger intense. Many came for prayer. I was completely astonished, however, as they paused to receive an offering designated for the poor of their community. In my estimation, these folks were poor themselves! But they saw far beyond their own situation and desired to help others in greater need.

I was deeply humbled as I reflected on the affluence of most people in North America. Although there is abundance, we are often unwilling to share with others. We will certainly give account before God for wastefulness, selfishness, and corruption of our society and our churches. Our hearts must be stirred to find ways to meet the genuine needs around us.

Psalm 121:1 begins, "*I will lift up my eyes to the hills.*" It's obvious that in order to look up to the hills, the writer was in the valley. The question is a cry: "*From whence comes my help?*" In this dark and lonely place, the valley was typical of trouble, discouragement— even hopelessness. There was a search for comfort, protection, and relief.

Then the author makes the matter-of-fact declaration. He knows the source of hope and help. He continues, "*My help comes from the Lord, Who made heaven and earth*" (Psalm 121:2). When our hearts search for solutions, for comfort, for an understanding friend remember the omnipotent God.

☙

Snuggle in God's arms. When you are hurting, when you feel lonely, left out. Let Him cradle you, comfort you, reassure you of His all-sufficient power and love.[24]

—Kay Arthur

[24] "18 Beautiful Quotes about Comfort," Christian Quotes, accessed September 25, 2018, https://www.christianquotes.info/top-quotes/18-beautiful-quotes-about-comfort/#ixzz5K9nLbC3w.

On occasion, I've experienced difficulty falling asleep. They tell me it has something to do with age! Recently, I had to get up early to drive nearly ten hours. I was in bed in good time, but sleep wouldn't come. I tried all the tricks: count sheep, cows, even dogs, cats, or rabbits. Get a drink of water. Go to the washroom. Read a book. Read the Bible. Get another drink. Pray. Sing. Make a sandwich. Eat the sandwich. Count the sheep again. Pray some more.

I thought about King David when he wrote Psalm 63:6–8:

When I remember You on my bed, I meditate on You in the night watches. Because You have been my help, therefore in the shadow of Your wings I will rejoice. My soul follows close behind You; Your right hand upholds me.

I could imagine David padding about his palace in the middle of the night, reflecting on the mercy and kindness of the Lord. As I shuffled down the hallway carpet, my own heart overflowed with gratefulness to God. I was indeed very thankful for all of God's blessings. I still couldn't sleep, but instead of sheep, now I counted God's blessings!

When I finally got up, I was tired before the day even started. I felt annoyed and aching from chasing sheep all night! However, after tanking up on several cups of strong coffee, I found the strength and necessary alertness. In fact, as the day passed, I actually felt somewhat refreshed.

By turning our hearts towards the Lord, remembering His love and care for us, we can find peace, courage, and strength in spite of difficulties or distress. God will faithfully keep us in His care.

The minor prophet Zephaniah makes this amazing statement in Zephaniah 3:17: "*The Lord your God in your midst, The Mighty One, will save; He will rejoice over you with gladness, He will quiet you with His love, He will rejoice over you with singing.*" Can we comprehend how the Almighty God delights in us? The thought brings fresh revelation of our intrinsic value as well as shows the unfathomable depths of His love. This verse even reveals that we make His heart sing with joy!

His supreme, creative purpose is that we likewise would find our greatest delight in Him. We also experience our deepest joy and greatest fulfillment in His presence. Let us respond to His great love by giving Him our hearts.

God loves each of us as if there were only one of us.[25]

—Augustine

---

[25] "21 Challenging Christian Quotes about God's Love," *One Thing Alone: Finding Joy in Jesus*, accessed September 25, 2018, https://onethingalone.com/christian-quotes-about-gods-love/.

Paul and Silas had been arrested while preaching the gospel. After being beaten, they were placed in a secure cell. It's not difficult to imagine their discomfort in that dungeon. There would be no food and little or no water. No doubt there were critters crawling about, including spiders, scorpions, or snakes! There would probably be an abundance of rats as well!

There would be no sanitation or toilets. The smell would be disgusting, the air hot, humid, and heavy. With their feet locked in stocks, they would be helpless to fend for themselves. Their response to this most uncomfortable situation, however, is astonishing and inspiring.

About midnight Paul and Silas were praying and singing hymns to God, and the prisoners were listening to them. Suddenly there was a great earthquake, so that the foundations of the prison were shaken; and immediately all the doors were opened and everyone's chains were loosed. (Acts 16:25–26)

Amazing things happen when we pray and sing praises to the Lord. Even in the most extenuating circumstances, we can find inexplicable peace, comfort, and freedom. If we concentrate on our problems, on people, or on ourselves, we will lose our song. But when Jesus is continually the center of our whole life, He will fill our hearts with a song of joy and praise—even in our darkest dungeons. As we proclaim God's goodness, others in prisons of darkness can hear the midnight song, giving them hope. They too can know the power of God to set them free.

In Isaiah 6:8, we read: *"Also I heard the voice of the Lord, saying: 'Whom shall I send, and who will go for Us?' Then I said, 'Here am I! Send me.'"* When he heard the Lord calling for someone to be His messenger and do His work, Isaiah willingly responded.

We may often feel inadequate or unqualified to accomplish God's plan and fulfill His purposes; however, if we willingly submit and obey, the Lord will do in us what we did not think possible. It may not be necessary to receive a specific call but rather to have a willingness to hear and obey God. As we take every opportunity to radiate God's love, He will accomplish His plan in our lives.

Faith never knows where it is being led, but it loves and knows the One who is leading.[26]

—Oswald Chambers

---

[26] "211 Quotes about Obedience," Christian Quotes, accessed September 25, 2018, https://www.christianquotes.info/quotes-by-topic/quotes-about-obedience/#ixzz5K9r3GMLK.

Together with friends, I walked towards the towering landmark. Rising several hundred feet above me was a major tourist attraction of the maritime town—a lighthouse. Situated near the entrance of the port, it had been built to direct ships safely into the harbor. The light keeper had lived nearby. His important responsibility was to make sure the light was always burning. For many years, these structures served to warn sailors of dangerous cliffs, submerged sandbars, or jagged rocks. Countless thousands of lives may have been spared because of the faithful, shining beams that gave direction, warning, and comfort.

The gospel of Christ is like a lighthouse. The Word of God offers direction to the safety of the harbor, warnings of destructive traps, and the comfort of God's love, peace, and eternal hope. Believers are light keepers. We have a great responsibility to keep the light and truth of the gospel shining brightly. As we live for Christ, we must take every opportunity to share the life-changing message—Jesus saves. Perishing souls can be rescued from the rocks of sin.

The light keeper had no way of knowing how many lives were saved, nor the far-reaching impact of his faithful work. He was only responsible to keep the light burning. We may never know the impact of God's light shining through us. Our part is to diligently obey the Lord, letting the gospel message radiate clearly in our lives. We leave the results with Him.

In Judges 6:14, God speaks to Gideon and tells him: "… *Go in this might of yours, and you shall save Israel from the hand of the Midianites. Have I not sent you?*" Gideon gave many excuses why he couldn't accomplish the task of engaging and winning the war with the Midianites. The Lord just told him to go with what he had and see what God would do. Although they were outnumbered by a ratio of 1 to 450, against impossible odds they won the war.

You may feel weak, insignificant, incapable, and unworthy, but the power behind you is greater than the task before you! You may not have a lot of strength, but as you step ahead in faith and obedience to the Word of God, doing what you can do, He will do what you cannot do.

❦

I am only one, but still I am one. I cannot do everything, but still I can do something; and because I cannot do everything, I will not refuse to do something that I can do.[27]

—Helen Keller

[27] "21 Awesome Quotes from Helen Keller," Christian Quotes, accessed September 25, 2018, https://www.christianquotes.info/top-quotes/21-awesome-quotes-from-helen-keller/#ixzz5K9vUhykw.

While driving on the Alaska Highway and other remote roads in the northwest, I was awed by the immensity of the Canadian wilderness. The magnificent forests, rivers, lakes, and mountain ranges stretch for thousands of kilometers. Although the forest extends beyond the horizon, it's made up of individual trees. A tree may be classed in one of several varieties and defined by its distinctive size, shape, and branch arrangement. Yet each tree is completely unique, the only one of its kind. Like snowflakes and fingerprints, each plant has its inimitable characteristics.

Most of the trees of these vast forests are never seen individually by a human being, yet they grow, maturing and reproducing according to God's command in Genesis. Unobserved, unpraised, they seek only to fulfil their destiny by daily lifting their branches in praise to God.

Perhaps you feel lost in a crowd: unnoticed, unappreciated, unknown. Like a tree in the forest, recognize your unique identity in Christ. Then pour your strength into showing the glory of God.

Chapter Four

PATIENCE IN PERSEVERANCE

The book of Nehemiah recounts the rebuilding of the walls of Jerusalem after the Jews returned from the Babylonian captivity. Nehemiah and those working with him faced tremendous obstacles. The enemies of Israel tried to get him to leave the work and meet with them in another place. They were planning to ambush him. It was a dangerous distraction. When that failed, they tried to fill him with fear, telling him he should hide in a secret place to protect himself.

As we follow God's way while accomplishing His work, we also must deal with similar conflicts. A multitude of distractions attempts to interfere with our relationship with Jesus. A thousand voices demand our attention. On the other hand, fears frustrate our efforts and keep us paralyzed. Nehemiah, however, worked steadily on. In a phenomenal fifty-two days, they had reconstructed the city wall! They took necessary precautions, and with perseverance they refused to be distracted from their purpose.

The Bible tells us in Numbers 23:19 that God does not lie or break His promises. We have all experienced broken promises, disappointed expectations, and undependable individuals. Even our most trusted confidents may let us down. The Word of God, however, reveals God's character. He is faithful; His promises are true. We can trust Him.

We must not become so preoccupied or dismayed with people or circumstances that we doubt God's ability to handle things in His own way and in His own time. What He said, He will bring to pass. Plant yourself firmly upon His Word and let His peace fill your heart.

As the people of God, we believe the word of God can be trusted in every way to speak what is true, command what is right, and provide us with what is good.[28]

—Kevin De Young

[28] "20 Quotes from DeYoung's 'Taking God at His Word,'" TGC: The Gospel Coalition, accessed September 26, 2018, https://www.thegospelcoalition.org/reviews/20-quotes-from-kevin-deyoungs-taking-god-at-his-word/.

The incoming tide washed over the rocks along the ocean shoreline. The water rose steadily until the breakers smashed against the towering granite cliffs. As I watched, the ocean spray lashed at rocks, the swirling froth rushing through crevices among the boulders. Although the colossal cliffs seemed invincible, the granite was being slowly eroded away. In the battle between rock and water, the water would eventually win—not by its strength, but by its tireless persistence.

Above the crashing waves, higher up the cliff, I noticed a large tree growing out of a crevasse in the solid rock. How could it survive in this precarious place? Obviously, many years before, a tiny seed had lodged in a crack of the rock. The germinated seed had sent miniscule rootlets into hairline fractures. Gradually the roots had enlarged, splitting the rock as the tree anchored itself firmly. By steady persistence, the life within the seed overcame the solid granite. Now the tree stood triumphant in this perilous location.

Both the tree roots and the wind-driven waves had discovered victory over the mighty granite—by simple perseverance. As we persist with patience, permitting the life of God's Word to grow within our hearts, we can rise triumphant in spite of seemingly impossible difficulties— thus we stand firm, solidly planted on the Word of God.

Abraham experienced the same human struggles we face. He had received the promise from God that a son, Isaac, would be born. He didn't immediately see the arrival of this child. In fact, he had to wait twenty-five years until both he and his wife were too old to naturally have children. Nevertheless, he tenaciously held on to his hope in God's promise. Paul says in Romans 4:18: "*who, contrary to hope, in hope believed, so that he became the father of many nations, according to what was spoken, 'So shall your descendants be.'*"

You also can steadfastly believe God's Word in the face of obstacles, impossibilities, and disappointments. Abraham's faith produced not only the child of promise, but the greater benefit—a profound relationship with God. Paul states it this way: "*Abraham believed God, and it was accounted to him for righteousness*" (Romans 4:3). By grace and through faith, we also can know this living relationship with Christ.

I believe in the sun
even when it is not shining.
And I believe in love,
even when there's no one there.
And I believe in God,
even when he is silent.[29]

—poem written by a Jewish prisoner in
a concentration camp

---

[29] "A Poem of Belief by a Jewish Prisoner in a Nazi Concentration Camp," *SAIRYD*, accessed September 26, 2018, https://sairyd.wordpress.com/2011/11/13/a-poem-of-belief-by-a-jewish-prisoner-in-a-nazi-concentration-camp/.

While reading on the deck and enjoying the sunshine, I was distracted by an ant crawling over my foot. It proceeded to make its way along a board then down through the grass. There were huge obstacles in its path: a deep crack in the boards, twigs, stones, grass roots, and even a brick. Intrigued, I watched as it searched for a clearer path.

The ant went one way then another, up and down, even backtracking, until it finally got past the barrier, only to find another difficulty in the way. Undaunted, it walked on, all six legs energetically carrying it towards some distant destination. Even when I picked up the twig it was on and put it in another place, with the same rigorous enthusiasm it found its place and kept on going.

Though the problems we face seem impossible and discouraging, keep walking on. The steady current of water proves stronger than the hardest rock, slowly wearing it away. Perseverance wins. We may have to backtrack, watch for different opportunities, or even try new routes; however, great mountains can be conquered as we keep reaching towards the goal. Paul says in Philippians 3:13–14: *"… but one thing I do, forgetting those things which are behind and reaching forward to those things which are ahead, I press toward the goal for the prize of the upward call of God in Christ Jesus."*

Babylon had defeated the nation of Judah. The capital, Jerusalem, had fallen; the temple had been destroyed. Now the citizens were captives in the foreign land, filled with despair. Through the prophets, the Lord had told the people of Judah that within seventy years He would bring them home again; however, in their distress it was easy to forget the promise of God. To add to their torment, their captors demanded they sing the beautiful songs of Israel. In Psalm 137:1–4,
we read their story:

> *By the rivers of Babylon, there we sat down, yea, we wept when we remembered Zion. We hung our harps upon the willows in the midst of it. For there those who carried us away captive asked of us a song, and those who plundered us requested mirth, saying, "Sing us one of the songs of Zion!" How shall we sing the Lord's song in a foreign land?*

Our extenuating circumstances may be heartbreaking, even seemingly hopeless. We wonder how we can find the strength to continue to worship, to sing praise to the Lord. We are not alone in our sentiments. Through the long, dark difficulties, remember the promises of God. As we walk on with Jesus, holding fast with patience, dawn will begin to unravel the canopy of darkness that enshrouds us.

He conquers who endures.[30]

—Persius

---

[30] "Top 80 Inspirational Perseverance Quotes and Sayings," Quote Ambition, accessed September 26, 2018, http://www.quoteambition.com/inspirational-perseverance-quotes-sayings/.

Iceland is an exceptional country. It has unique history, geography, and stunning scenery. Hardy inhabitants have carved the island into a successful, modern society. During several visits, it has been my privilege to minister in a number of towns and villages around the island. On one occasion, arrangements had been made for me to speak in a village accessible only by a road through a mountain tunnel.

This tunnel was eight kilometers long but only one lane wide—just large enough for one truck to pass through. Every five hundred meters, a small side-lane was available in case we met someone. The speed limit was about forty kilometers per hour. There was little light. Remember, of course, this is an island known for earthquakes and volcanoes!

As we entered the tunnel, I realized how small and dark it was. I'm sure my eyes were large like dinner plates. I don't like tunnels through mountains at the best of times, but this was another dimension of fright! For a good part of the trip, I kept my eyes glued on the rock walls visible in the headlights. When we saw the lights of an approaching vehicle, the experienced driver quickly squeezed into the side-lane. We all sucked in our breath until the other vehicle squeaked past. The rest of the time, I prayed with my eyes shut! It was great preparation for the service later that day! In the tunnel, however, I discovered that the courageous Icelanders had placed the greatest encouragement possible. Attached to the sides of the tunnel were small signs with two numbers. The top number was the distance traveled; the bottom, how far we had yet to go.

The first sign had the number one over the number seven. We had just begun the journey: one kilometer down, seven more to travel. When it was four over four, we knew we were in the center of the earth! Finally, it was seven over one—just one kilometer to go! We knew we were just about out of the darkness. With bated breath, we watched for the light at the end of the tunnel. What joy and relief to make it through—until I remembered we had to return by the same route!

As you pass through the tunnels of difficult experiences, keep traveling on in the light you have. There are signposts marking the promises and presence of God. Patiently persevere. In God's perfect time you shall arrive in the light of day.

In Colossians 1:10, we see an excellent summary of the believer's purpose: "*that you may walk worthy of the Lord, fully pleasing Him, being fruitful in every good work and increasing in the knowledge of God.*" It's not really a sacrifice to do even difficult acts of service for those whom we love deeply. How much more it is our joy to serve Jesus Christ in righteous thoughts and actions as our expression of love for Him.

A man of ill-repute told Napoleon Bonaparte: "We have the same name," to which Bonaparte retorted, "Then live up to the name or change it!" We have the tremendous privilege to know Christ and to carry the name of Jesus in our hearts. God's Word challenges us to live in such a way that His name is honored. We need Jesus to be the center of all our aspirations. May our thoughts be filled with Him, and our lives continually reflect His glory.

❧

I will love the light for it shows me the way, yet I will endure the darkness for it shows me the stars.[31]

—Og Mandino

[31] "Uplifting Quotes for Difficult Times," Keepinspiring.me, accessed September 26, 2018, http://www.keepinspiring.me/uplifting-quotes-for-difficult-times/#ixzz5KE34OauC.

One of my friends is a gifted horticulturist. Her home is filled with flourishing plants. She loves to explain the history of each one and tell the secrets of its care. Among her selection, she has several tropical plants that, in their native environment, would flourish in the jungle.

If plants could think and feel, imagine the sentiments of these tropical plants upon their arrival in Canada in the middle of winter! They would shiver at the sight of snow. The cold would give them goosebumps—or whatever bumps plants get! The dry atmosphere of forced-air furnaces would wilt and curl their leaves. But given just a little care, water, light, and fertilizer, these plants created for the tropical jungle are able to thrive in the living room of an environmentally-hostile, foreign land. In the same way, we can also choose to make our world a better place by blooming where we are planted.

In Genesis, we read the story of Jacob's favorite son, Joseph, who was sold by his brothers into Egyptian slavery. Through the many painful circumstances, God was with him and blessed him. Eventually he became the prime minister of Egypt. In Genesis 41:52, he explained that he named his second son Ephraim because "… *God has caused me to be fruitful in the land of my affliction.*"

When we review Joseph's life story, we can learn how to flourish in spite of rejection, pain, and difficulties.

• Forgive those who cause suffering.
• Forget past anguish.
• Focus on the present situation.
• Follow after excellence in service to God and fellow man.

There was a beautiful shade tree growing in my yard. In the spring, I noticed that several branches didn't produce leaves. Then some of the new leaves began to wither. On close inspection by a specialist, it was discovered that the tree was diseased and dying. It would have to be cut down. Perhaps it will grow again if the root is healthy. If the root is diseased,
the tree is lost.

The Bible gives us warnings to take care of our hearts. In Proverbs 4:23, we find the admonition to *"Keep your heart with all diligence, for out of it spring the issues of life."* If our hearts are filled with evil, sin will eventually corrode our minds and destroy our souls. If we let the Lord cleanse us, good fruit will pervade our lives and bring comfort to others also.

∞

The proof of spiritual maturity is not how pure you are but awareness of your impurity. That very awareness opens the door to grace.[32]

—Philip Yancey

[32] "25 Quotes about Purity," Christian Quotes, accessed September 26, 2018, https://www.christianquotes.info/quotes-by-topic/quotes-about-purity/#ixzz5KE9VgERA.

The enormous branches of a cottonwood poplar tree stretched across the path, bringing shelter and shade to passers-by. Birds flitted among its leaves. I was in awe of its height and beauty as I walked along the path. As I came closer, however, I noticed a narrow but deep gash descending several meters down the tree. Even from the distance where I was standing, I could look into the opening and observe the inside of the tree. To my astonishment, the interior was filled with decaying wood. It would only be a matter of time before this forest giant would tumble, disintegrating on the ground.

How could it be? It looked so powerful. It obviously had endured generations of winds, storms, heat, and cold. Yet soon it would literally collapse. Although it looked healthy on the outside, the heart of the tree had been destroyed by disease and insects.

What a lesson for us! Our lives, our homes, our churches, our nations may have appearances of strength and vitality—but if the internal integrity and character are rotten, ultimate destruction is sure to come.

With many distractions vying for our attention, it's easy to lose focus on the most important values of life. Jesus, however, tells us the secret of contentment and fulfillment: *"But seek first the kingdom of God and His righteousness, and all these things shall be added to you"* (Matthew 6:33). We must choose to let Jesus have priority over all details of our lives. When He is the source of profound satisfaction for our souls, everything else in life will fall into place.

The major value in life is not what you get. The major value in life is what you become.[33]

—Jim Rohn

33 "The Best Quotes about Value," Ranker, accessed September 26, 2018, https://www.ranker.com/list/notable-and-famous-value-quotes/reference.

I have a friend who lives with his wife and two sons in a large city. To help instill a good work ethic in his young sons, they purchased two pigs that were kept on a plot of land outside the city. They spent every weekend caring for the animals. Their father reminded them, however, that these pigs were being raised for food, so they shouldn't get too attached to them. To help keep that point clear, they named them "Bacon" and "Sausage!" Since then, I've wondered if the day came when the children would ask, "Are we eating Bacon or Sausage today?"

We also need to keep proper perspective, not becoming too attached to the materialism and pleasures of this world. They shall soon pass away. The apostle Paul says in 2 Corinthians 4:18: *"while we do not look at the things which are seen, but at the things which are not seen. For the things which are seen are temporary, but the things which are not seen are eternal."* Let's center our hearts on timeless principles that shall be ours forever.

The apostle Peter knew difficult times were ahead for the followers of Christ. He wrote:

> *Beloved, do not think it strange concerning the fiery trial which is to try you, as though some strange thing happened to you; but rejoice to the extent that you partake of Christ's sufferings, that when His glory is revealed, you may also be glad with exceeding joy.* (1 Peter 4:12–13)

Peter reminds us not to be surprised by the trials of life. Although we don't like problems, he tells us to rejoice, knowing through these difficulties we can partake of Christ's sufferings. There's a place of intense joy through identity with Christ. There are lessons of trust, surrender, and faith that can only be learned through tribulations and the discomforts of life experiences.

Do not fear the conflict, and do not flee from it; where there is no struggle, there is no virtue.[34]

—John of Kronstadt

[34] "20 Encouraging Quotes about Trials and Struggles," Christian Quotes, September 26, 2018, https://www.christianquotes.info/top-quotes/20-encouraging-quotes-trials-struggles/#ixzz-5KE7w4yrC.

The Bible recounts the story of Job. In a matter of days, he lost all of his material possessions, his extensive wealth, and his family. Then he lost his own health. Those who came to comfort him only added to his grief and sorrow, condemning and accusing him. Heartbroken, sick, and feeling very alone, he couldn't understand all the trouble that had befallen him. In spite of it all, he retained his integrity, declaring his trust in God. In the end, God blessed Job more than previously, proving His sovereignty to him and his friends.

In the middle this great trial, Job made a profound confession of his trust in God:

> *For I know that my Redeemer lives, and He shall stand at last on the earth; and after my skin is destroyed, this I know, that in my flesh I shall see God, whom I shall see for myself, and my eyes shall behold, and not another. How my heart yearns within me!* (Job 19:25–27)

What a powerful declaration of hope in the face of great tragedy!

Perhaps troubling circumstances are happening in your life. In a place of despair, focus on the promises of His Word. The Lord will renew your faith and courage with the assurance of unshakable hope in Christ.

The power of God is never limited by our circumstances. In moments we may be overwhelmed by what we perceive as impossibilities and disappointments, but at the end of human ability, God still does His supernatural work. Our responsibility is to watch, pray, and trust in Him.

Reminding himself of God's faithfulness, David wrote:

I would have lost heart, unless I had believed that I would see the goodness of the Lord in the land of the living. Wait on the Lord; be of good courage, and He shall strengthen your heart; wait, I say, on the Lord! (Psalm 27:13–14)

Hold fast. God is at work. Someday His great masterplan will be revealed.

Many of life's failures are people who did not realize how close they were to success when they gave up.[35]

—Thomas A. Edison

[35] "Tenacity Quotes," AZ Quotes, accessed September 26, 2018, http://www.azquotes.com/quotes/topics/tenacity.html.

My friend was sharing with me the effectiveness of her recent carb-free diet. After avoiding pasta and bread for nearly a month, she had been able to lose a significant amount of weight. Her husband, intrigued by her success, had recently decided to join her.

He enthusiastically participated in our conversation. "I haven't eaten any bread since Monday when I started this diet too," he stated. Then with a reflective expression he queried, "By the way, what day is today?"

"Tuesday," she replied with a burst of laughter!

Sometimes the dark nights of temptation, disappointment, or trial may feel endless and overwhelming—when in reality they are temporary and transitory. Victory demands perseverance, discipline, and courage. The apostle Paul declared in Ephesians 6:13–14: "*Therefore take up the whole armor of God, that you may be able to withstand in the evil day, and having done all, to stand. Stand therefore ...*" Tenacity is necessary to achieve desired results.

In the Amplified Bible, we read in Hebrews 4:16:

Therefore let us [with privilege] approach the throne of grace [that is, the throne of God's gracious favor] with confidence and without fear, so that we may receive mercy [for our failures] and find [His amazing] grace to help in time of need [an appropriate blessing, coming just at the right moment].

This scripture reminds us that we can come before the throne of God with our requests—whatever they may be. In His time and in His way, He will provide the mercy, the grace, and all the help we need. He knows more about our circumstances than we do! What a powerful promise! What a tremendous assurance! Let us bring our burdens and cares to God in prayer and then walk on with new strength, facing the challenges ahead.

Be sure your feet are in the right place, then stand firm.[36]

—Abraham Lincoln

---

[36] "Tenacity Quotes," AZ Quotes, accessed September 26, 2018, http://www.azquotes.com/quotes/topics/tenacity.html.

As I walked along a small, rock-strewn mountain trail, a flash of color caught my eye. The clump of flowers was almost completely hidden from view among the rocks. I went to inspect it more closely. The vibrant, cheerful colors were a sharp contrast to the dry grass and grey rock. Fragile petals glistened with dew in the crisp air. Far from rushing crowds of city streets, obscure and alone beside a forgotten path, these beautiful wildflowers did what they were created to do: bloom faithfully.

We're all given responsibilities, created and called by God to fulfill the destiny He has planned. There are those who must live in the glare and glamour of the city lights; others are chosen to bloom in obscurity, cheering the lonely and forgotten corners of the world. Whatever the path God has set before us, He will supply the resources and courage. We must faithfully live for His glory alone. We bring life and grace to the corner where we are planted.

Chapter Five

SHELTER IN OUR SHADOWS

The prophet Jeremiah was deeply distressed because God had revealed calamities that would soon befall the nation of Judah. His heart was broken because of the sin and rebellion of his people. In his anguish, however, he remembered God's unfailing mercy: *"Through the Lord's mercies we are not consumed, because His compassions fail not. They are new every morning; great is Your faithfulness. 'The Lord is my portion,' says my soul, 'Therefore I hope in Him!'"* (Lamentations 3:22–24).

That Bible passage inspired the familiar old hymn, "Great is Thy Faithfulness," written by Thomas Obadiah Chisholm:

> Pardon for sin and a peace that endureth,
> Thine own dear presence to cheer and to guide;
> Strength for today and bright hope for tomorrow,
> Blessings all mine with ten thousand beside!
> Great is Thy faithfulness …[37]

---

[37] "Great Is Thy Faithfulness," *Wikipedia*, last modified June 25, 2018, https://en.wikipedia.org/wiki/Great_Is_Thy_Faithfulness.

What hope, security, and confidence we have knowing our lives are in God's hands. We can be filled with gratitude for the Lord's faithfulness, mercy, and grace.

In Psalm 63:1, we get a glimpse of David's intense love for the Lord. It begins, "*O God, You are my God; early will I seek You; my soul thirsts for You; my flesh longs for You ...*" In verse eight he adds, "*My soul follows close behind You; Your right hand upholds me.*" This song was written in the desert while fleeing from those who were trying to harm him. Surrounded by enemies, distractions, and frustrations, David turned his heart to God. From the depths of his soul, he poured out his worship—his heart passionately pursued the Lord.

Look above the turmoil and chaos that presses against you. Be renewed in love and devotion to God. Let your soul hunger and thirst to exalt Him. Be revived and refreshed as you express your adoration to Christ.

છ

Come, Lord, stir us up and call us back. Kindle and seize us. Be our fire and our sweetness. Let us love. Let us run.[38]

—Augustine of Hippo

[38] Aaron West, "20 Inspiring Quotes about Worship," Mediashout, March 13, 2017, accessed September 26, 2018, https://www.mediashout.com/inspiring-worship-quotes/.

It was a heavy, hot, humid day in a tropical country. I was perspiring profusely, not unlike being inside a sauna! As I walked along the street, I had visions of ice cubes bobbing on the surface of a large glass of lemonade. Turning the corner, I came into the deep shadow of a tall building. Instantly, the cooler air and the slight breeze brought relief. Other folks had already made the discovery and were leaning against the building or sitting on the curb. Everyone was seeking relief from the sultry heat. I paused to lean a moment against the wall. How refreshing! How soothing! I found new courage to face the heat and to finish my journey.

Being hunted in the desert by King Saul, David understood the relief and comfort of a sheltered place. But he also had made a great discovery: "*God is our refuge and strength, a very present help in trouble*" (Psalm 46:1).

We must take a break away from the pressures of life to run into the eternal refuge—the presence of God. We need to take time to absorb His love and His Word. Then we will be strengthened to run on and finish strong. Isaiah spoke this promise: "*But those who wait on the Lord shall renew their strength; they shall mount up with wings like eagles, they shall run and not be weary, they shall walk and not faint*" (Isaiah 40:31).

We often find ourselves in difficult situations where there seems to be no solution. We may even feel trapped, not knowing how to disentangle ourselves from complicated circumstances or conflicts. The Lord has promised to direct our steps as we put our trust in Him. In the Bible, David also found himself in perilous struggles, but he recognized the Lord's amazing intervention: "*Our soul has escaped as a bird from the snare of the fowlers; the snare is broken, and we have escaped. Our help is in the name of the Lord, who made heaven and earth*" (Psalm 124:7–8).

Whatever your circumstances, put your trust in the Lord and seek His solutions. Like David, you will look back with thanksgiving, knowing God has brought you through.

☙

Faith is taking the first step even when you don't see the whole staircase.[39]

—Martin Luther King Jr.

[39] "18 Powerful Quotes about Trust," Christian Quotes, accessed September 26, 2018, https://www.christianquotes.info/top-quotes/18-powerful-quotes-trust/#ixzz5KFCZ5pVO.

The mother hen was scratching the ground, contentedly clucking to her chicks. Eight tiny, yellow balls of fluff followed her closely, carefully checking for grubs each time she paused on freshly stirred soil. As they crossed the chicken pen, they kept their distance from the rest of the flock. Mother hen kept a wary eye out for danger.

When the farmer's dog came around the corner, immediately her urgent call brought the chicks running to her. Quick as a flash, every chick dove under her overshadowing wings. Little beaks and bottoms could be seen poking out here and there from under Mother's feathers as they huddled in the safest place they knew. After the dog wandered past, the hen ruffled out her feathers, and the brood continued their scratching expedition. As evening fell, she led them all into the chicken coop. They nestled again under her wings—warm, cozy, and safe.

In Psalm 91:1–4, we read these heart-warming words:

He who dwells in the secret place of the Most High shall abide under the shadow of the Almighty. I will say of the Lord, "He is my refuge and my fortress; my God, in Him I will trust." Surely He shall deliver you from the snare of the fowler and from the perilous pestilence. He shall cover you with His feathers, and under His wings you shall take refuge …

When the pressures of life are overwhelming, we can run to the refuge—our eternal Savior. In Christ we find comfort, courage, and confidence.

The disciples were confused, wondering why Jesus was washing their feet. It was customary for servants to do this work—but He was their Master. They could not yet comprehend the principle of service to others; therefore, He gave them this promise in John 13:7: "*What I am doing you do not understand now, but you will know after this.*"

We may have many questions about experiences in our lives. We may wonder why we pass by difficult trials. Let us place our trust in God not only for the blessings He brings to us, but for who He is. Soon we will understand God's eternal plan. Until then, we will love Him, trust Him, and leave the unanswered mysteries in His hands.

Trust the past to God's mercy, the present to God's love, and the future to God's providence.[40]

—Augustine

[40] "18 Powerful Quotes about Trust," Christian Quotes, accessed September 26, 2018, https://www.christianquotes.info/top-quotes/18-powerful-quotes-trust/#axzz5K9mxwunT.

The story has been told of two men who lived sometime during the sixteenth century. They were ministers of the gospel who had been imprisoned for their faith in Christ and had been condemned to death. In their prison cell, on the night before they were to be burned at the stake, the younger man was very agitated. He cried out in fear and despair: "At all costs I must not deny my Lord! How will I be able to endure this! When the flames surround me and the pain becomes severe, how will I stay true to Christ?" He momentarily held his hand in the flame of the burning candle. With horror, he drew it back. "Oh, how shall I make it through?"

The older man sat quietly writing letters, listening to the anguish of his younger companion. Finally, he spoke comfort, saying, "My friend, tonight you do not need the grace to die. But tomorrow, in the trial of fire, you will have all the grace you need."

As our anxious hearts contemplate the troubled days about us—as we consider the difficulties we may face—we understand the dread and anguish of this young man. The apostle Paul, however, shared the secret of God's sustaining grace. He tells his story in 2 Corinthians 12:7–9:

> And lest I should be exalted above measure by the abundance of the revelations, a thorn in the flesh was given to me, a messenger of Satan to buffet me, lest I be exalted above measure. Concerning this thing I pleaded with the Lord three times that it might depart from me. And He said to me, "My grace is sufficient for you, for My strength is made perfect in weakness." Therefore most gladly I will rather boast in my infirmities, that the power of Christ may rest upon me.

God has looked at our tomorrows. He has measured His grace for our circumstances. He confirms, "My grace is sufficient for you" (2 Corinthians 12:9).

In Habakkuk 2:3, the Lord reminds the prophet that what He has spoken will come to pass: *"For the vision is yet for an appointed time; but at the end it will speak, and it will not lie. Though it tarries, wait for it; because it will surely come, it will not tarry."* In our impatient modern world, we can be tempted to doubt God's Word when we don't receive instant answers to our prayers or see the fulfillment of scripture as we had anticipated.

The apostle Peter also penned a warning about the days to come. He foretold of a time when people would be so entangled in their distractions that they would be unprepared for Christ's return. In the busy occupations of our lives, rest assured God's promises will come to pass. May we occupy ourselves in fulfilling His highest purposes.

$$\text{\textit{CB}}$$

The beautiful thing about this adventure called faith is that we can count on Him never to lead us astray.[41]

—Chuck Swindoll

---

[41] "18 Powerful Quotes about Trust," Christian Quotes, accessed September 26, 2018, https://www.christianquotes.info/top-quotes/18-powerful-quotes-trust/#axzz5K9mxwunT.

I had arrived at the new location late the night before. Now early in the morning when I looked out the window, a dense fog covered the entire landscape. Although I'd been told the view was magnificent, I had no way of knowing—except to believe what they told me and imagine what it looked like. For nearly two days, we lived under the dense blanket of darkness and humidity.

Then one morning bright sunshine streamed through my window. I was speechless! Now I could see what the cloud had been hiding. Majestic mountains encircled a sparkling lake. Clusters of vineyards dotted the valley below.

Through the dark moments of life, our hearts and minds may be shrouded in the fog of confusion and uncertainty; however, we have the promises of God's Word and the comfort of His presence. We may not see the way or understand His plan, but we can hold fast to His promises. We keep walking on, trusting His faithfulness. The clouds will roll away; the sun will shine again.

In Psalm 139:1–2, David recognizes that God is infinitely interested in his life: "*O Lord, You have searched me and known me. You know my sitting down and my rising up; You understand my thought afar off.*" In difficult moments, we can be reminded that the Lord knows the intricacies of our lives. He hears the cries of our hearts before they are even uttered. He knows our struggles and our failures; He knows our victories and our joys. He understands our thoughts, our motives—even when we don't understand our own minds! He knows the total truth about us. And He loves us still.

⌘

I have not failed. I've just found 10,000 ways that won't work.[42]

—Thomas A. Edison

[42] "Thomas A. Edison Quotes," BrainyQuote, accessed September 26, 2018, https://www.brainyquote.com/quotes/thomas_a_edison_132683.

Although the hospitality was gracious, I was challenged by the elegance of the meal. I was the guest in an affluent home. The table was prepared with upper class sophistication. As we sat together enjoying the lovely food, I felt somewhat self-conscious handling the two knives and three forks. Trying to act cool to impress, I was following every rule of etiquette I had ever learned!

It was all so delicious. I daintily took one of the small, bright, red tomatoes and popped it into my mouth. I bit into it. The juicy little critter sprayed liquid clear across the entire table, hitting everything—and everyone—in its path! I was aghast! Embarrassed—an understatement!

My dear host and hostess began to laugh! Wiping tomato juice off their plates, their faces, even the milk and margarine containers, they merrily carried on. Mortified, I was for once speechless! As for impressions—this one would be unforgettable! Then I, too, had to laugh.

I am deeply grateful for the kindness of friends who love me in spite of myself! Even greater is the grace of God, who looks beyond my faults to see my need. He knows who we think we are, who we want others to think we are, and who we really are. Yet He loves us still, ever drawing us closer to Himself.

Political turmoil, national upheavals, and unexpected military activity have created fear, uncertainty, and insecurity everywhere. How very grateful we can be for the rock of peace and hope— Christ Jesus. In Psalm 40:2–3, David describes God's mercy lifting him from hopelessness into security: "*He also brought me up out of a horrible pit, out of the miry clay, and set my feet upon a rock, and established my steps. He has put a new song in my mouth—praise to our God …*" In the middle of the most difficult circumstances, we can experience the abiding peace of His presence: "*But the Lord has been my defense, and my God the rock of my refuge*" (Psalm 94.22).

Because of the empty tomb, we have peace. Because of His resurrection, we can have peace during even the most troubling of times because we know He is in control of all that happens in the world.[43]

—Paul Chappell

---

[43] "19 Beautiful Quotes about God's Peace," Christian Quotes, accessed September 26, 2018, https://www.christianquotes.info/top-quotes/19-beautiful-quotes-about-gods-peace/#ixzz5PlkUtSny.

While standing on the shore of a lake on a windy afternoon, I watched unusually large waves rushing furiously towards the shore. As they crashed on the nearby rocks, rolling up the sandy beach, they seemed to stretch with all their might to swallow up the land. They tried with all their strength to reach beyond the outlines of the shore. I was suddenly reminded of the scripture in Jeremiah 5:22:

> *"Do you not fear Me?" says the Lord. "Will you not tremble at My presence, Who have placed the sand as the bound of the sea, by a perpetual decree, that it cannot pass beyond it? And though its waves toss to and fro, yet they cannot prevail; though they roar, yet they cannot pass over it."*

Although all the forces of darkness may seem to be arrayed against us—reaching to destroy and discourage—this scripture reminds us that God's decrees rule over all. The enemy is powerless to harm us when we are sheltered in the rock, Christ Jesus.

In Colossians 3:2, we are commanded: *"Set your mind on things above, not on things on the earth."* These words challenge us to live with our priorities firmly based in lasting values. This is diametrically opposed to the mentality of the present society.

Although possessions and finances are important parts of daily life, they must never hold our hearts. Corrie Ten Boom once said, "Hold everything in your hands lightly, otherwise it hurts when God pries your fingers open."[44] Life at best is fleeting. Temporal. Uncertain. Let Jesus hold your deepest affections. He is our secure and eternal inheritance.

His will is our hiding place.[45]

—Corrie Ten Boom

---

[44] "Corrie ten Boom, Quotes," goodreads, accessed September 26, 2018, https://www.goodreads.com/quotes/28322-hold-everything-in-your-hands-lightly-otherwise-it-hurts-when.

[45] "Security," Daily Christian Quotes, May 22, 2008, accessed September 26, 2018, https://www.dailychristianquote.com/tag/security/.

I had just invited everyone in the service to stand and join me in singing the chorus of the hymn "How Great Thou Art." Then I noticed several people pointing to the curtains, which were moving as though being blown by a strong wind. Behind me the large projector screen began swaying. My notebooks slid across the pulpit. Several people sat down abruptly. I continued to sing but was greatly distracted by all the motion in the room. What was happening?

My first thought was that we may be experiencing a manifestation of God's presence, like on the day of Pentecost! A vague sense of dizziness swept over me. The whole building was moving! I realized this was an earthquake. Later it was confirmed. Even though we were six hundred kilometers from the epicenter, we had felt the shock of the 7.7 earthquake, one of the strongest in Canadian history for that region.

We experience the sense of ultimate insecurity when the very earth on which we stand cannot be trusted. Humans play their political games, pretentiously, arrogantly boasting of their achievements. But with one shake, they are brought to the realization of their frailty and their mortality. The material possessions, the pride, the pomp, and the popularity can be destroyed so rapidly. There is absolutely no security outside of a personal relationship with Jesus Christ. In Him our soul is forever safe.

Although the book of Revelation has been the source of varied theological interpretations and speculations, the basic theme is unmistakable: Jesus Christ shall ultimately reign as the eternal Sovereign. As we observe the clash of kingdoms, it's clear that efforts of humanism fail miserably to resolve the conflicts of good and evil. What peace and assurance to know God has everything under control! He is our everlasting shelter. When we put our faith and trust in Jesus Christ, our hope is sure in Him as we anticipate His soon return. With the apostle John we say, "... *come, Lord Jesus*" (Revelation 22:20).

For the Christian, heaven is where Jesus is. We do not need to speculate on what heaven will be like. It is enough to know that we will be forever with Him.[46]

—William Barclay

[46] "14 Inspiring Quotes about Heaven," Christian Quotes, accessed September 26, 2018, https://www.christianquotes.info/top-quotes/14-inspiring-quotes-about-heaven/#ixzz5KFhxyhxL.

Many express shock and horror in the destructive wake of earthquakes, volcanoes, hurricanes, and tornadoes. Such disasters are reminders of the awesome powers that can be unleashed by nature. Within seconds, entire nations can be shaken ... literally! Isaiah reminds us of this truth:

Behold, the nations are as a drop in a bucket, and are counted as the small dust on the scales; look, He lifts up the isles as a very little thing ... All nations before Him are as nothing, and they are counted by Him less than nothing and worthless. (Isaiah 40:15, 17)

We are often guilty of pride and independence, which are basic premises of humanistic deification. However, the prestigious political titles, material wealth, pomp, and prejudice that promote human pride will all dissipate into dust. Observing these catastrophes should quickly restore humility before Almighty God. We are utterly and completely dependent upon His mercy and grace.

Chapter Six

DELIVERANCE IN THE DARKNESS

Wanting to capture the prophet Elisha, in the middle of the night the enemy circled the city in which he lived. When his servant awoke and saw they were surrounded, he was very frightened. In 2 Kings 6:16–17, we read Elisha's response:

> "… Do not fear, for those who are with us are more than those who are with them." And Elisha prayed, and said, "Lord, I pray, open his eyes that he may see." Then the Lord opened the eyes of the young man, and he saw. And behold, the mountain was full of horses and chariots of fire all around Elisha.

When we look from God's viewpoint, the immense obstacles shrink into obscurity. He sees the beginning and the end. He knows every aspect of our present circumstances. Let's ask Him to allow us to view our crisis from His perspective. As we change our focus to see situations through His eyes, we discover His unlimited resources and receive new courage.

Jesus said in John 14:27: "*Peace I leave with you, My peace I give to you; not as the world gives do I give to you. Let not your heart be troubled, neither let it be afraid.*" This promise has never changed. In a world of distractions and distresses, our hearts can find peace, comfort, and courage as we lift our thoughts to Him.

The apostle Paul declared: "*Be anxious for nothing, but in everything by prayer and supplication, with thanksgiving, let your requests be made known to God; and the peace of God, which surpasses all understanding, will guard your hearts and minds through Christ Jesus*" (Philippians 4:6–7). When our hearts feel overwhelmed, we can experience peace that cannot be explained by simply turning to His unchanging promises.

☙

God cannot give us a happiness and peace apart from Himself, because it is not there. There is no such thing.[47]

—*C. S. Lewis*

---

[47] "Peace with God Quotes," AZ Quotes, accessed September 26, 2018, http://www.azquotes.com/quotes/topics/peace-with-god.html.

The ministry schedule included a drive of several hours northeast of Quebec City, traveling along the coast of the Gulf of St. Lawrence. I had been told I was about to see spectacular scenery; however, the day of my journey was filled with heavy rain and dense fog. As I slowly counted nearly five hundred kilometers along the tortuous, winding route, I had only insignificant glimpses of the forests and rocks along the way. Concentrating on the few meters of road I could see, my impression was of nothing but the endless twists and turns of the highway.

Fortunately, my return took place on a bright, sun-bathed day. What a difference! I was amazed by the beauty that had completely eluded me previously. The height of the cliffs and the density of the forest astounded me. I was extremely glad I had driven prudently on the hairpin curves—particularly when I saw the sheer drop-offs into the water below! It reminded me of a verse of the familiar song "Amazing Grace," written by John Newton:

> Through many dangers, toils and snares,
> I have already come.
> 'Tis grace hath brought me safe thus far
> And grace will lead me home.[48]

In the darkness, the fog, and the difficult moments of life, we may not be conscious of the protecting, merciful hand of the Lord guiding us. It is only later we realize His great faithfulness in directing us, even when we didn't know the dangers. At last we understand the purpose and the beauty of the trials we have passed through.

---

[48] John Newton, "Amazing Grace," Timeless Truths, accessed September 26, 2018, http://library.timelesstruths.org/music/Amazing_Grace/.

The turmoil around the world is disturbing. The most distressing crises, however, are those within our immediate sphere. The daily circumstances of our family and friends can be far more pressing than the tragedies, wars, and disasters in other people's lives, whether locally or in distant places.

Perhaps you are pre-occupied with situations that seem unending and overwhelming. The beautiful promise given in Psalm 55:22 is like fresh water to a thirsty soul: "*Cast your burden on the Lord, and He shall sustain you; He shall never permit the righteous to be moved.*" Take hold of His promise and abandon your cares to Him

Pray, and let God worry.[49]

—Martin Luther

[49] "21 of the Most Inspirational Quotes about Trusting God," jonbeaty.com, accessed September 26, 2018, https://www.jonbeaty.com/21-of-the-most-inspirational-quotes-about-trusting-god/.

In Daniel 3, we read the inspiring story of Daniel's three friends, Shadrach, Meshach, and Abednego. Along with all the other governors of Babylon, they were commanded to bow before the golden image set up by King Nebuchadnezzar. They refused to bow to this idol. They would not compromise their commitment to the God of Israel, even though they were threatened to be burned in an overheated fiery furnace. Their answer to the king in Daniel 3:17–18 is a powerful statement of faith in God:

> *If that is the case, our God whom we serve is able to deliver us from the burning fiery furnace, and He will deliver us from your hand, O king. But if not, let it be known to you, O king, that we do not serve your gods, nor will we worship the gold image which you have set up.*

The furious king had them arrested, bound, and then thrown into a furnace heated seven times hotter than normal. His bruised ego was seeking to destroy any challengers to his power. After some moments, we're told he looked down into the fire, probably hoping to see the charred remains of these men who spoke of the God higher than himself. To his amazement, the three men were walking about in the flames, and there was another man with them! He cried out with astonishment. He wasn't destroying them—they were multiplying! The Lord brought them safely through the flames without even the smell of smoke upon them.

We recognize the unlimited power of God to bring deliverance in our difficulties. However, the commitment of these three men to God was not determined by the outcome— rather, the outcome was determined by their commitment! Their devotion to God was undeterred by the possibility of death itself. Let's be steadfast and abandon ourselves in submission to Christ, in spite of our circumstances.

In 2 Corinthians 9:8, we have the wonderful promise of God's sufficient grace for every situation in life: *"And God is able to make all grace abound toward you, that you, always having all sufficiency in all things, may have an abundance for every good work."* God's grace is more than enough.

Stress and panic pervade our society. The pressures of decisions and dilemmas cause discouragement and despair. The well-loved hymn "What a Friend We Have in Jesus" reminds us of the "peace we often forfeit and the needless pain we bear, all because we do not carry everything to God in prayer."[50]   Hebrews 4:16 tells us that we can *"… come boldly to the throne of grace, that we may obtain mercy and find grace to help in time of need."*

If your heart is heavy, troubled, or distressed, take it all to Jesus. In simple prayer, lay your burdens at His feet. Take hold of His promise of grace sufficient for every need.

Anxiety's like a rocking chair. It gives you something to do, but it doesn't get you very far.[51]

—Jodi Picoult

---

[50] Joseph M. Scriven, "What a Friend We Have in Jesus," Timeless Truths, accessed September 26, 2018, http://library.timelesstruths.org/music/What_a_Friend_We_Have_in_Jesus/.

[51] "Anxiety Quotes," goodreads, accessed September 26, 2018, https://www.goodreads.com/quotes/tag/anxiety.

After a wonderful service, I joined the family where I was lodging. Together we stayed up to watch the evening news. It's never a good idea to watch the news just before going to bed! That broadcast included the horrific account of an entire family killed by a psychopath.

Later as I tried to sleep, fear-filled thoughts raged within my mind. What if I were attacked? What if I have no money? What if I get sick? What if something happens to my friends or family? Questions poured into my head—all of them prefixed with "What if?" Many nights for nearly two years following that incident I struggled with tormenting thoughts and anxieties.

One day a friend prayed with me about this situation, and in an instant the torment was gone; however, the same day I saw a phrase on a calendar that changed my life. It stated: "God does not give us grace for our imaginations, but for our experience." That day I made a tremendous discovery. I had called on the Lord for comfort and protection in all my fears. I suddenly realized God could not help me—because nothing was happening! There was no crisis; there was no danger, only in my imagination!

Someone said that 98 percent of the things we worry about will never happen, and the 2 percent that does happen never happens the way we planned! We don't buy clothes for our shadows. Why not? Because our shadow isn't reality. If I'm wearing clothes, my shadow is fairly decent! God will not waste His grace on my imaginations; however, scripture does promise: "... *my God shall supply all your need according to His riches in glory by Christ Jesus*" (Philippians 4:19). In the actual crisis I find protection, provision, comfort, and courage in Christ. He is my eternal hope and refuge. He is enough.

In Matthew 14:30–31, Peter stepped out of the boat to join Jesus walking on the stormy waves, but "…*when he saw that the wind was boisterous, he was afraid; and beginning to sink he cried out, saying, 'Lord, save me!' And immediately Jesus stretched out His hand and caught him* …" As long as Peter focused on Jesus, he could experience the impossible and live a miracle. When his attention was diverted from Jesus, Peter lost the capacity to walk on the water.

When Jesus is the center of our life, the pivot of our purpose and our focus, His grace empowers us to overcome overwhelming obstacles. We are easily distracted from Jesus, however, and the impossibilities and distresses of life seem to swallow our hope. Like Peter, we must call upon Jesus, refocus priorities, surrender to the Lord, and let Him take control. He may not take away the storm, but He will give us the strength to walk with Him through it.

Most of us spend too much time on what is urgent and not enough time on what is important.[52]

—Stephen R. Covey

[52] "Priorities Quotes," goodreads, accessed September 26, 2018, https://www.goodreads.com/quotes/tag/priorities.

One of my friends trained as a pilot. During the lessons, the teacher incessantly reminded the students to know the instrument panel of their aircraft. He often repeated the instructions to trust the instruments—no matter what the circumstances. Later, my friend was flying a small, single engine airplane between two cities: Lethbridge, Alberta and Saskatoon, Saskatchewan. He left in the bright sunshine of a winter day; however, about nightfall, he encountered a powerful winter storm.

The aircraft shook and shuddered, trembling in the wind. As the night settled down, the horizon became invisible because of the driving snow. In the turbulence, my friend quickly became disoriented. He was sure the aircraft was plunging and losing altitude. Gripping the controls with near panic, he was convinced a crash was inevitable. But the altimeter was normal. He forced himself to concentrate on the instrument panel and remember the instructor's commands.

For a few startling minutes, he had the sensation the plane was spiraling. The sentiment was so strong, he found himself leaning over in the cockpit. Still, the instruments said all was well. Finally, perspiring and trembling, he began to wonder where he was. Perhaps he was lost. He could see nothing. He tried to get a radio response.

Then a calm voice from the control tower responded: "We have you on our radar. You are coming in right on schedule. Just hold your course." The plane descended through the clouds in the darkness. Then he saw the lights of the runway. The instruments had brought him safely through.

In spite of the turbulence of your troubled world, the principles and the promises of the Word of God will bring you safely home. Remain faithful. Hold fast. He will bring you through the storm.

In Hebrews 10:23–25, we find an admonition of tremendous relevance to us today:

Let us hold fast the confession of our hope without wavering, for He who promised is faithful. And let us consider one another in order to stir up love and good works, not forsaking the assembling of ourselves together, as is the manner of some, but exhorting one another, and so much the more as you see the Day approaching.

Every voice around us may bring discouragement. The night seems long; the answer appears far away. But don't give up. The answer may be closer than you think. More than ever, walk in obedience and perseverance, keeping your heart burning with passion for Jesus.

☙

To talk with God, no breath is lost. Talk on! To walk with God, no strength is lost. Walk on! To wait on God, no time is lost. Wait on![53]

—E. Stanley Jones

[53] "Walking with God Quotes," AZ Quotes, accessed September 26, 2018, http://www.azquotes.com/quotes/topics/walking-with-god.html.

The ancient adage states: "The darkest hour is just before the dawn." The Bible account of David provides an excellent illustration of this truth. As a boy he had been anointed King of Israel, but for about fifteen years there seemed to be no sign of this promise coming to pass. Then, in an unexpected attack, the enemy had stolen his wives and children and those of his soldiers.

David was in grave danger. In their deep distress, even his own men turned against him. It was devastating: *"Now David was greatly distressed, for the people spoke of stoning him, because the soul of all the people was grieved, every man for his sons and his daughters. But David strengthened himself in the Lord his God"* (1 Samuel 30:6).

After passing through this moment of great darkness and despair, suddenly, within hours, everything changed. They conquered their enemy; their families were restored. King Saul was killed in battle, and the nation called for David to lead the country. David had no way of knowing during the deep difficulty that within three days he would be crowned king.

Perhaps you're passing through a dark moment now. Discouragement and distress seem to overwhelm you. Take heart. This moment of difficulty may be positioning you to fulfill God's highest purposes for your life. Keep hanging on to God's promise; keep your heart fixed on His Word. You may be closer to the answer than you realize. The darkest hour may be nearly past. A new day is dawning.

There are many parallels between the nation of Judah in the time of the prophet Jeremiah and the day in which we live. Good is called evil, and evil is called good. Dishonesty, treachery, immorality, and debauchery are found acceptable, even entertaining, while righteousness and integrity are difficult to find. In Jeremiah 17:9, the prophet declares: "*The heart is deceitful above all things, and desperately wicked; who can know it?*" Repentance, surrender, and obedience to Christ are the only cures for sinful hearts. Only He can transform the innermost part of our being. Now is the time to recognize our need and walk totally committed to Jesus.

The less Holy Spirit we have, the more cake and coffee we need to keep the church going.[54]

—Reinhart Bonnke

---

[54] "Commitment to God Quotes," AZ Quotes, accessed September 26, 2018, http://www.azquotes.com/quotes/topics/commitment-to-god.html.

Once sin and rebellion were permitted to enter the perfect world God had created, humanity rapidly descended into violence and immorality. The judgment and destruction of the wicked was imminent. In the middle of this chaotic distress, the Lord found one man who lived righteously, choosing to obey God. In Genesis 6:8, we read: *"But Noah found grace in the eyes of the Lord."* That one man was instrumental to bring hope and redemption for all who would enter the ark God had provided.

For over 120 years, as he built the ark in obedience to God's instructions, Noah preached and prepared, warning the people of impending doom. Few listened. When the order was given, Noah and his family, together with the animals, entered the safety of the ark.

The rain began to fall. Too late, the world realized the reality of God's warning. No doubt they rushed to enter the ark, but now the door was closed. Although many may have begged Noah to open the door, he could not—for God had shut the door. They perished because they would not repent and submit to the Lord when He was calling out to them through Noah.

Around us today we also see broken lives caused by the people's choices to rebel against God; however, the Lord has provided a place of hope and security—relationship with Jesus Christ. The door of mercy still stands open. When we heed His voice, we can enter into the secret place of the Most High and find our hiding place under the shelter of His wings (Psalm 91:1).

In 2 Kings 19, the Assyrian army sends threatening letters to the godly King of Judah, Hezekiah. Very afraid of this massive army, Hezekiah lays the letters before the Lord and prays for God's mercy upon his nation. God supernaturally intervenes, and thousands of the invading forces suddenly die. Against all odds, the Assyrian army turns tail without attacking Judah. What army captain in his right mind wouldn't leave after waking up in the morning to 185,000 corpses, dead from a mysterious cause? The nation is spared.

Sometimes we may feel hopeless and helpless, but we can pray with faith, knowing that God is at work. Our limitations are God's possibilities! The answer may not come when or how we expect, but our trust is in His unlimited power.

Our high and privileged calling is to do the will of God in the power of God for the glory of God.[55]

—J. I. Packer

---

[55] "Power of God Quotes," AZ Quotes, accessed September 26, 2018, http://www.azquotes.com/quotes/topics/power-of-god.html.

The mid-week service had been arranged at a remote town. About two dozen folks gathered in the church basement for the Bible study and fellowship. I was sharing some thoughts about Paul and Silas in the Roman dungeon at Philippi: their physical difficulty, their pain, and their discomfort. Their feet were in stocks, preventing movement. They would be hungry and thirsty. Rats would be crawling in the place.

I saw several folks suddenly distracted by something behind me. A mouse had found a hole near the door and had chosen that exact moment to make his entrance. Talk about an illustrated sermon! There were more than a few gasps, and a couple of women hastily climbed on the chairs. Two or three brave men found a broom to chase the poor critter back out the door.

Like the mouse, sin will take every opportunity to creep into our lives—even into our churches! We need to quickly and efficiently recognize it and show it the door. If we excuse it, soon there will be a whole nest of trouble.

The people of Israel had rebelled against the Lord. Their activities and idolatry had placed them outside of His protection. Now they were experiencing great trouble. The prophet expresses his amazement at the callousness of their hearts—even in face of calamity: We read in Isaiah 64:7: "... *there is no one who calls on Your name, who stirs himself up to take hold of You; for You have hidden Your face from us, and have consumed us because of our iniquities.*"

As spiritual darkness and apathy attempt to numb our souls in these perilous days, we need to turn to the Lord with tender hearts to seek His mercy and grace. We must stir ourselves to take hold of God. Now, more than ever, we need Him to direct our way.

ༀ

The power of God will take you out of your own plans and put you into the plan of God.[56]

—Smith Wigglesworth

---

[56] "Power of God Quotes," AZ Quotes, accessed September 26, 2018, http://www.azquotes.com/quotes/topics/power-of-god.html.

The nation of Judah was facing annihilation by the Babylonian empire. Prophets, including Ezekiel, had repeatedly warned them of impending doom, but only a handful of folks were listening. In fact, very few even seemed alarmed. They were complacent, willfully ignoring their sin and rejecting the need for national repentance. Speaking through the prophet, the Lord says in Ezekiel 22:30: *"So I sought for a man among them who would make a wall, and stand in the gap before Me on behalf of the land, that I should not destroy it; but I found no one."* This scripture expresses the Lord's grief when He could find no one willing to intercede for the nation. Not only was there rebellion and rejection of God's principles, but even those who professed to know Him had grown lethargic and apathetic. No one seemed to care.

This world will also soon face a great day of reckoning. God will deal with the pride and arrogance of humanity. Now is the time for every believer to seek the Lord and ask Him to grant repentance, mercy, and salvation. We can stand in the gap by interceding in prayer for those who are lost and without hope.

God revealed to the prophet Daniel intricate historical details that would happen hundreds, even thousands, of years in advance. Isaiah foretold the rise of Cyrus, King of the Medes, who would become the conqueror and ruler of Babylon more than one hundred years before Cyrus was even born—even naming him!

We are assured that God has a great and eternal purpose for the world as well as for our personal lives. We read in Romans 8:28, "... *we know that all things work together for good to those who love God, to those who are the called according to His purpose.*" This scripture assures us our lives are part of a great and eternal plan. As we put our faith in the Lord, He is working in us to make something beautiful that will bring glory to Him. Although we don't understand much of the big picture, we trust and obey Him.

Trust God to weave your thread into the great web, though the pattern shows it not yet.[57]

—George Macdonald

[57] "18 Powerful Quotes about Trust," Christian Quotes, accessed September 26, 2018, https://www.christianquotes.info/top-quotes/18-powerful-quotes-trust/#axzz5K9mxwunT.

Corrie Ten Boom often used the illustration of a tapestry to explain how God works things together for good in our lives. Using a poem credited to Grant Colfax Tuller, she presented the working side of a woven tapestry. Tangled colors and threads were a jumble, a mess, almost resembling a disaster. But then she turned it over. The other side was absolutely beautiful!

> My life is but a weaving between my God and me,
> I do not choose the colours, He works so steadily.
> Oft times He weaves in sorrow, and I in foolish pride,
> Forget He sees the upper, and I the underside.
> Not till the loom is silent, and the shuttles cease to fly,
> Will God unroll the canvas, and explain the reason why.
> The dark threads are as needful in the Weaver's skillful hand,
> As the thread of gold and silver in the pattern He has planned.[58]

When Joseph was rejected and sold by his brothers to be re-sold in the slave markets of Egypt, his heart must have been broken— torn with confusion and despair. Then, falsely accused by a wicked woman, he was cast into the Egyptian prison. Everything looked hopeless. Forgotten by friends, forsaken by family, and forced into horrible circumstances, he kept his integrity and his faith in God. He trusted that the Lord would fulfill His promises to turn the situation around.

Suddenly, in a sovereign turn of events, Joseph became the prime minister of Egypt. Later, when his brothers came to the land in search of food, he understood why he had walked such a difficult road. It had been the master plan of God. Joseph found himself in exactly the right place, speaking the Egyptian language, understanding the foreign culture, in a powerful political position. He was now able to protect and provide for the people of Israel in the time of great famine. Far more important, however, Joseph's

---

[58] "Life is a Tapestry," *Beneath My Heart,* accessed September 26, 2018, http://www.beneathmyheart.net/2016/01/life-is-a-tapestry/.

position assured the coming Messiah through the house of Israel, the descendant of Abraham—exactly as God had promised. The fulfillment of this promise reaches to us today. We can receive salvation and eternal life through Jesus Christ, because God's promises are sure!

At this moment, your life may be filled with tangles of despair. Everything looks dark and meaningless. Rest in this assurance— God is at work. Someday you will see the other side of the tapestry. Then you will see that the biggest knots in your life were the finest points of stitch in the finished picture.

The children of Israel were suffering hard bondage as slaves in Egypt. With desperation they cried out to the Lord for deliverance. It seemed that God had forgotten His promise to them. Year after year they saw no answer, but in Exodus 2:24–25 we read: "*So God heard their groaning, and God remembered His covenant with Abraham, with Isaac, and with Jacob. And God looked upon the children of Israel, and God acknowledged them.*"

As we read the full story, we discover that God has been personally implicated in preparing their answer for eighty years! Moses had been born, grown, and groomed to lead the people out of Egypt. Their deliverance was already on the way! We must not despair; the answer to our prayer may be nearer than we think.

The greatest tragedy of life is not unanswered prayer, but unoffered prayer.[59]

—F. B. Meyer

---

[59] "Answered Prayers Quotes," AZ Quotes, accessed September 26, 2018, http://www.azquotes.com/quotes/topics/answered-prayers.html.

Many years ago, on one of my first mission trips, I traveled alone to Brazil. I had written the missionaries with whom I expected to stay, informing them of my flight arrival time in a nearby city. However, when I arrived late in the evening, there was no one to meet me. Puzzled and somewhat unnerved, I finally went to a hotel. Being inexperienced in international travel, I had neglected to take telephone numbers or street addresses, a necessity I discovered too late.

As I looked out of the hotel window across the major metropolis, I had the terrifying thought that I could just disappear. They would say at home, "She went to Brazil and we never heard of her again!" It was hard to settle down for the night with thoughts like that in my head! After some panic prayer, I fell asleep.

I awakened early in the morning with a plan. Sitting in the lobby of the hotel, I asked everyone who came near if they spoke English. Finally, a handsome young man entered and acknowledged he could speak a little English. I explained my dilemma. All I had was the postal box number and the name of the town where the missionaries lived. My plan was to get to that post office, which was in a town thirty kilometers away, find the street address, and arrive at the home of the missionary. In retrospect, I realize it was a completely crazy idea!

He looked closely at my information. "The bus does not go there. The taxi would be too expensive," he said. Then with a bright smile, he looked at me and with a strong accent declared, "Me take you!" The thought briefly passed through my mind that if I was going to disappear, it may as well be with a handsome, young man!

Very kindly, this amazing gentleman drove me to the town. After inquiries at the post office, he delivered me safe and sound to the missionary's home. They had never received my letter! They were also preparing to leave for a three-day ministry journey. If I had arrived fifteen minutes later, I would have been in an enormous pickle! God is faithful to watch over us, even when our innocence or ignorance is downright dangerous!

Chapter Seven

PRESSING TOWARDS THE PRIZE

The sprinters line up at their blocks. Every nerve is alert. Anticipation is palpable. The starting gun is fired. In a flash the competitors are off—racing for the finish line.

We're all in the race of life. God has given us a track to follow, a course to complete. The start is important, but the finish is crucial. The apostle Paul was able to give this valedictory as he faced the end of his life:

> *I have fought the good fight, I have finished the race, I have kept the faith. Finally, there is laid up for me the crown of righteousness, which the Lord, the righteous Judge, will give to me on that Day, and not to me only but also to all who have loved His appearing.* (2 Timothy 4:7–8)

We may not experience world acclaim. We are called to simply follow Jesus with faith and obedience. One day, we shall all stand before God. On that day of reckoning, we shall give account for the race we've run. It will be eternal success to hear

His voice of approval, "*Well done, good and faithful servant* ..." (Matthew 25:21). The goal of every believer is to run strong and finish well.

I peeked through the door into the church auditorium. The pastor had requested I speak with the young people of the church. I had been delighted with the opportunity; however, when I saw the room filled with nearly forty teenagers, I began to have second thoughts. They were all between twelve and twenty years old. How would I keep their attention?

I picked up my electric guitar and began to sing, hoping to catch their attention with a lively gospel tune. It worked. All eyes were on me. Then I overheard one excited boy about fourteen years old whisper with astonishment, "Look, you guys! The old lady plays electric guitar!"

Time waits for no man, and not many women either! Billy Graham once said his most astonishing discovery about life was its brevity. Short-term waiting seems to go by slowly, but the long-term flashes past. Yesterday is gone; tomorrow has not yet come. Recognizing the transience of life, let us live today with eternity in view.

Middle age is when work is a lot less fun and fun is a lot more work.[60]

—Laurence J. Peter

---

[60] Quotefancy, accessed October 1, 2018, https://quotefancy.com/quote/1364514/Laurence-J-Peter-Middle-age-is-when-work-is-a-lot-less-fun-and-fun-is-a-lot-more-work.

We had enjoyed dinner together before starting the Sunday afternoon service. The building was warm. The chairs were comfortable. The crowd was small. Several folk were struggling to stay attentive. The temptation to nap was strong. I was trying my best to keep the people awake with an interesting message. A man sitting on the front seat began looking at his watch. Then he took it off and, holding it up higher, made some adjustment to it.

Reminded of the story of a similar event, I started to laugh and told the man I didn't mind him looking at his watch, but would be pleased if he didn't shake it to see if it had stopped. Everyone laughed and came alive again, but then the gentleman innocently responded, "I wasn't checking the time; I was checking the date!" At that response, we all nearly came unglued! I assured him it was still Sunday afternoon!

It's amazing how minutes spent waiting seem to drag on for an eternity, but years appear to pass in the blink of an eye: "*As for man, his days are like grass; as a flower of the field, so he flourishes. For the wind passes over it, and it is gone, and its place remembers it no more*" (Psalm 103:15–16). Time is a precious commodity. Every passing second is a moment we will never see again. Let's make an eternal difference today.

Spring is a beautiful season. The lengthening days, the melting snow, the swelling buds assure us of warmer days to come. In the same way, Jesus stated we could recognize the signs marking His soon return. When the fig tree blossomed, He said, we would know summer is coming.

There are startling signs that the world systems as we know them may soon collapse. Fear and uncertainty are everywhere; however, in Luke 21:28, Jesus says, "*Now when these things begin to happen, look up and lift up your heads, because your redemption draws near.*" We must prepare our hearts, being attentive to hear and obey His voice.

When He returns is not as important as the fact that we are ready for Him when He does return.[61]

—A. W. Tozer

[61] "Preparing for Jesus' Return Quotes," goodreads, accessed September 26, 2018, https://www.goodreads.com/work/quotes/18940727-preparing-for-jesus-return-daily-live-the-blessed-hope.

The day was breezing past with dozens of activities planned. A neighbor had passed on, and I was hurrying to accomplish a multitude of tasks before attending the funeral. It's never wise to hurry to a funeral! I made an accidental misstep and found myself on the ground with a sprained ankle. It wasn't too serious, but it demanded the use of crutches for nearly a week—which definitely cramped my style! I was extremely grateful that the ankle healed very quickly. My activities could resume at full speed again.

Experiences of this sort definitely enlarge our ability to empathize with others who may be suffering. It also served as a reminder of how quickly our situations may be altered. Life at best is uncertain. In a moment, all can be swept away. Jesus Christ offers the rock-solid assurance, comfort, and guidance that can hold us firm during the tragedies and upheavals of this changing world.

In the book of Acts, we read the history of the early church and the travels of the apostle Paul. He experienced much persecution and pressure. His entire purpose and passion, however, was to proclaim the good news of Jesus. Although his life was in constant danger, his focus was fixed on the eternal prize. Facing imprisonment, he stated in Acts 20:24:

> *But none of these things move me; nor do I count my life dear to myself, so that I may finish my race with joy, and the ministry which I received from the Lord Jesus, to testify to the gospel of the grace of God.*

May we not be distracted by the materialism, turmoil, and despair of our present world but keep clearly focused on God's priorities.

There are no crown-wearers in heaven who were not cross-bearers here below.[62]

—Charles Spurgeon

[62] "14 Inspiring Quotes about Heaven," Christian Quotes, accessed September 26, 2018, https://www.christianquotes.info/top-quotes/14-inspiring-quotes-about-heaven/#ixzz5KFii6BPd.

Recently, I met a man who had been converted to Christ in a country hostile to Christianity. He shared how for months he had been imprisoned, beaten, tortured, and finally able to miraculously escape. Now he assists others in these perilous places, offering comfort, advice, and resources.

On one occasion, after interrogation and brutal mistreatment, his captors informed him they would send in dogs to tear him to pieces. He was in great pain and weary of it all. He cried out to the Lord for strength. To his relief, the dogs, which had been trained to attack and kill, refused to touch him! His tormentors were shocked! As God had shut the mouths of the lions for Daniel, He had calmed the dogs to protect His faithful servant.

Recent statistics regarding the persecution of Christians worldwide reveal that approximately 135,000 people a year are martyred because of their faith in Christ. In other words, about every five minutes, someone, somewhere is been killed because they are a Christian. Increasingly, we see media mocking and muzzling evangelical believers.

Jesus clearly told us that if the world hated Him, it would also hate those who follow Him:

Blessed are those who are persecuted for righteousness' sake, for theirs is the kingdom of heaven. Blessed are you when they revile and persecute you, and say all kinds of evil against you falsely for My sake. Rejoice and be exceedingly glad, for great is your reward in heaven, for so they persecuted the prophets who were before you. (Matthew 5:10–12)

It doesn't bring glory to God to be persecuted for our own foolishness, lack of tact, or un-Christ-like behavior. However, when we have walked in obedience and humility yet are maligned and misunderstood for Christ's sake, we must seek to bless those who curse us and love those who hate us. Perhaps others will understand His love and come to know Jesus as their Savior.

Everywhere we see the chaos of a rebellious and sin-sick world. We can become stressed by the cares and selfish indulgence of society. In the middle of the mess, however, we must change our focus and look again at the eternal promise. In Revelation 21:1–4, John describes what God has prepared for those who love Him:

> *Now I saw a new heaven and a new earth, for the first heaven and the first earth had passed away. Also there was no more sea. Then I, John, saw the holy city, New Jerusalem, coming down out of heaven from God, prepared as a bride adorned for her husband. And I heard a loud voice from heaven saying, "Behold, the tabernacle of God is with men, and He will dwell with them, and they shall be His people. God Himself will be with them and be their God. And God will wipe away every tear from their eyes; there shall be no more death, nor sorrow, nor crying. There shall be no more pain, for the former things have passed away."*

What tremendous hope we have! Jesus Himself is preparing a place for us to be forever with Him.

I would rather go to heaven alone than go to hell in company.[63]
—R. A. Torrey

---

[63] "14 Inspiring Quotes about Heaven," Christian Quotes, accessed September 26, 2018, https://www.christianquotes.info/top-quotes/14-inspiring-quotes-about-heaven/#ixzz5KFh1hMBA.

The first house I purchased was a sixty-five square meter mobile home. This type of house was very cheaply constructed, but affordable. Fixed up, it was a very cute nook. Although it was small, it was adequate for my needs at the time; however, after a few years, more space became necessary.

I had always been quite content with my friendly, comfy home. I was sure I would miss the cozy snugness of its tiny rooms when I moved. The new location was four times the size and a ranch-style bungalow. The first night after the excitement of the move, I padded from room to room on the carpeted floors. I was amazed at God's provision. This new home was much more spacious and comfortable ... a dream come true. I never missed my little, old mobile home for one second.

We live in the beautiful creation that God has made, surrounded by various material luxuries. Enjoying the company of friends and family, heaven can seem very far away. The thought of the transition to our eternal home may seem sad, even unwelcome, as we busy ourselves with the pleasures and business of earthly life.

One day we will cross the great divide separating time from eternity. Believers will discover the place Jesus promised to be far superior, beyond our wildest dreams. The wonder of His presence will make the most celebrated pleasures of earthly life seem like insignificant dust. We shall rejoice in the light of His glory forever.

In the first chapters of Revelation, Jesus addresses seven Asian churches. He speaks affirmation as much as possible, but He also gives very sharp warnings regarding their immorality and idolatry—calling them to repentance. In Revelation 2:4, Jesus says, *"Nevertheless I have this against you, that you have left your first love."* The Lord was deeply grieved because they had lost their passion and fervent love for Him.

These words should startle, convict, and challenge us. Have we cooled in our passion for Christ? Would these words be true of us also? Have we grieved the heart of God by our complacency? Do we prefer the distractions of this world over a relationship with Him? May we come to Jesus with true repentance stirring our hearts, seeking Him.

❧

We always keep God waiting while we admit more importunate suitors.[64]

—Chazel

[64] "Distractions," Daily Christian Quotes, September 30, 2011, accessed September 26, 2018, https://www.dailychristianquote.com/tag/distractions/.

I wasn't in a particular hurry to get to the airport. I already had my ticket and reservation, so it would be a breeze to pick up my boarding pass and board the plane. However, I had not taken into account the morning rush hour traffic, the lineup at security, or the queue at the passport control. With seconds to spare, I raced down the corridor, sped onto the gliding sidewalk, and zipped through my gate, breathlessly diving into my seat on the airplane. I was the last one to board. The door was closed and we were ready for takeoff. I had just about missed the flight!

On many occasions, Jesus spoke of His second coming, illustrating His message through parables as well as quoting passages from the Old Testament scriptures. He continually warned the disciples to always be watching and waiting for Him, working tirelessly with great anticipation.

After the resurrection of Jesus, a bewildered group of followers watched Him ascend into heaven. Two angels appeared, saying to them: *"Men of Galilee, why do you stand gazing up into heaven? This same Jesus, who was taken up from you into heaven, will so come in like manner as you saw Him go into heaven"* (Acts 1:11). These words have brought challenge, courage, and confidence to every generation of Christians as we have waited with expectancy and hope.

How much nearer we are now! His return may be imminent. We need to heed His warnings as He commands His people in Luke 21:34–36:

> *But take heed to yourselves, lest your hearts be weighed down with carousing, drunkenness, and cares of this life, and that Day come on you unexpectedly. For it will come as a snare on all those who dwell on the face of the whole earth. Watch therefore, and pray always that you may be counted worthy to escape all these things that will come to pass, and to stand before the Son of Man.*

We need to be ready to depart at any moment—prepared to meet the Lord.

Grain ready to harvest is collected, threshed, and winnowed by a combine. It's then transported and stored in granaries until shipped to market. It's the culmination of a farmer's season of labor. Seeds that were sown several months before have germinated and multiplied. They will be used for food in various forms. The sale of the grain will supply for the needs of the farmer, and the food will benefit the world.

There's something fascinating about the harvest, for it produces both reward and regret. There is reward because the season's work is over. There may also be regret because the work may have been done more efficiently.

Every day we plant seeds. What will the harvest bring? Let us be diligent; then we will rejoice in the reward and not experience regret.

If you don't like what you are reaping, you had better change what you have been sowing.[65]

—Jim Rohn

[65] "34 Inspirational Quotes on Reaping and Sowing," Awaken the Greatness Within, accessed September 26, 2018, http://awakenthegreatnesswithin.com/34-inspirational-quotes-on-reaping-sowing/.

The doors of the large elevator opened just as we arrived in front of them. Quickly, we followed those who boarded. Along with others pushing buttons for various floors, we pressed the one for the sixth floor. To our chagrin, however, we had failed to notice this elevator was descending first to the fourth floor below ground, which led to the parking area! In our haste, we had followed the crowd downwards. It demanded patience, but soon enough we began our ascent, eventually arriving at the destination we desired.

Upon reflection, I thought of many individuals who are following the crowd through life. Some people yield to the influence of their friends, supposing it will lead to more pleasure or satisfaction. Others are caught in their selfishness or rebellion. Many put their trust in religiosity without true faith in Christ. Everyone hopes eventually to go up to heaven at the end of their lives. How horrible to discover that they had made wrong choices! To arrive in a hopeless eternity from which there is no escape! The scriptures teach this principle in Proverbs 14:12: "*There is a way that seems right to a man, but its end is the way of death.*"

Now is the time to prepare to meet with God. Be certain you will be going the right direction when you die. Make sure you are on the right boat before you leave the harbor.

We can see the quagmire of human hopelessness on every newscast. Troubling world events reveal we may be closer to Christ's return than we imagine. The apostle Peter assures us that as we wait for the Lord's return, God continually calls, patiently waiting for hearts to turn to Him. In 2 Peter 3:9, we read: "*The Lord is not slack concerning His promise, as some count slackness, but is longsuffering towards us, not willing that any should perish but that all should come to repentance.*"

Now is the time to prepare our hearts to stand before the Lord. Let us live with humility and repentance, laying aside every distraction, making Christ the center of who we are and what we do.

❧

My home is heaven. I'm just traveling through this world.[66]

—Billy Graham

---

[66] "Heaven Sayings and Quotes," Wise Old Sayings, accessed September 26, 2018, http://www.wiseoldsayings.com/heaven-quotes/.

A dear elderly friend died recently. Her passing away brought sadness, as I will miss her cheerful laugh and faithful friendship. However, death is a reality of life. We mourn those we miss. There is finality as the curtain falls and the door is closed. There are footsteps we will never hear again. The voice is silenced; the touch is cold. How precious is the hope we have in Christ! Jesus says in John 14:1–3:

> *Let not your heart be troubled; you believe in God, believe also in Me. In My Father's house are many mansions; if it were not so, I would have told you. I go to prepare a place for you. And if I go and prepare a place for you, I will come again and receive you to Myself; that where I am, there you may be also.*

There is a place of no more tears, no more pain, no more fear, no more need. We have the promise to be with Jesus forever. It is the special place prepared for those who have submitted their lives to Him. It is for those who have received His grace for repentance and faith for salvation.

There are many responsibilities, activities, and distractions that constantly demand our time and attention. It can be a challenge to juggle our minutes, to invest our time for maximum profit. In Psalm 90:12, Moses prays, *"So teach us to number our days, that we may gain a heart of wisdom."*

Time is probably our most valuable unrenewable resource. We all have the same number of minutes and hours in each day, but we never know when the last shall come. As we reflect on the brevity of life, as well as the nearness of our Lord's return, may we wisely spend our allotted time.

Heaven is not a figment of imagination. It is not a feeling or an emotion. It is not the "Beautiful Isle of Somewhere." It is a prepared place for a prepared people.[67]

—Dr. David Jeremiah

---

[67] "Heaven Sayings and Quotes," Wise Old Sayings, accessed September 26, 2018, http://www.wiseoldsayings.com/heaven-quotes/.

Having traveled almost constantly during the last four decades, I've learned a few things about preparations for a journey. The most important part of the voyage, however, is to know where you are going! Some people spend months saving and planning for elaborate vacation tours or family expeditions. Others travel routinely for business enterprises.

Unfortunately, multitudes of people are soon going on an eternal journey with no thought of their destination—and for which they have made no preparation. Jesus says in Matthew 7:13–14:

> *Enter by the narrow gate; for wide is the gate and broad is the way that leads to destruction, and there are many who go in by it. Because narrow is the gate and difficult is the way which leads to life, and there are few who find it.*

The Bible makes it clear there is a heaven to gain and a hell to shun.

Now is the time to get our destination confirmed and our ticket in order through repentance and faith in Christ. The call for our departure may come at any moment.

The Gift of Salvation

If you have never given your life to Christ, I earnestly urge you to surrender to Him today. According to Romans 3:23, "... *all have sinned and fall short of the glory of God.*" The Bible tells us that peace with God is received by turning to Him from our sins:

> ... *if you confess with your mouth the Lord Jesus and believe in your heart that God has raised Him from the dead, you will be saved. For with the heart one believes unto righteousness, and with the mouth confession is made unto salvation ... For "whoever calls on the name of the Lord shall be saved."* (Romans 10:9–10, 13)

You can receive His life now by repentance and faith. Pray this simple prayer:

> *Lord, I know I have sinned. I believe You are the Son of God and that You died on the cross to forgive my sins. I believe You have risen from the dead with power to give me a transformed*

life. Please forgive me, change my heart, and set me free. I surrender the control of my will to You. Help me to follow You. In Jesus' Name. Amen.

Read the Bible and pray every day. Find others who love Jesus who can help you to follow Him. Jesus will lift you from the darkness of sin; He will set you on a solid rock and fill your heart with a new song of praise. Let Him be the center of your life.

FOR MORE INFORMATION,
PLEASE CONTACT:

Inspiration Ministries

Box 44

Margo, SK Canada S0A 2M0

www.inspirationministries.net

Conclusion

We are surrounded by a society imperiled by chaotic insecurity. Our post-modern civilization, which has resisted God's principles of truth and refused His absolutes, flounders in the rubble of fallen sand castles. Without the foundation of God's Word, hearts are hopeless, corroded by selfishness, crumbling in despair. However, with faith in Christ and the assurance of His promises we stand firm on the solid rock.

The Sovereign Designer has a divine plan directing the details of our lives. He gives value to every life and purpose for every circumstance. His great hand is orchestrating our steps, even in the darkness. We cannot explain, nor even understand, how songs of hope and praise to God rise in our soul in spite of sorrow, disappointment, or discouragement. From the infinite source of His mercy, we find grace to persevere in hardship as we patiently pursue solutions. When pressures seem ready to consume us, we discover the secret place near to the heart of God. He is the refuge we run into. There, surrounded by His peace, we find the courage to travel on. Sometimes unexpectedly, a door of deliverance opens. We discover a clearer path through the shadows.

The people of Israel had endured the dark sorrow of their deportation, then seventy years of captivity in Babylon. Throughout the troubled times, God had directed, comforted, and sheltered them. At last came the day of liberation. They could return to their homeland. Their song of grief was turned to melodies of praise:

> *When the Lord brought back the captivity of Zion, we were like those who dream. Then our mouth was filled with laughter, and our tongue with singing. Then they said among the nations, "The Lord has done great things for them." The Lord has done great things for us, and we are glad.* (Psalm 126:1–3)

Although the night may seem unending, we trudge on. The song of faith in Christ still stirs within. We press forward. Soon the shadows will break into glorious day.

PRODUCTS AVAILABLE FROM INSPIRATION MINISTRIES:

BOOKS

Above the Storm

Joy in the Journey

Choose to Live Life

Choose a Changed Mind

Choose a Contented Heart

MUSIC CDs

Collection of Favorites

Collection of Favorites #2

The Timeless Prize

For a complete catalogue of Anita's music, CDs, DVDs,
and other ministry information please visit her website at

www.inspirationministries.net

AND ORDER YOURS TODAY!